Start RIGHT MARKETING

The Business of Making an *Impact*

TRACY REPCHUK

Also from Tracy Repchuk

 *31 Days to Millionaire Marketing Miracles*

The Poetry of Business

 *Quantum Leap Your Life*

Ultimate Life Lessons

 *25 Brilliant Business Mentors*

Ready, Aim, Inspire

Discover the power in these titles at:
www.TracyRepchuk.com/book

Start Right Marketing
The Business of Making an Impact

Tracy Repchuk

Co-authored with

Jim Meskimen • Fantastic Frank Johnson
MarBeth Dunn • Canon Wing • Michele Camacho
Susie Garcia • Alberto Liberal • Sam Rafoss
Nadine Lajoie • Teresa de Grosbois • Margo DeGange

Splendor Publishing
College Station, TX

SPLENDOR PUBLISHING
Published by Splendor Publishing
College Station, TX.

First published printing, September 2014

Copyright © Tracy Repchuk, 2014
All Rights Reserved

No part of this book may be used, reproduced, uploaded, stored or introduced into a retrieval system, or transmitted in any way or by any means (including electronic, mechanical, recording, or otherwise), without the prior written permission of the publisher, with the exception of brief quotations for written reviews or articles. No copying, uploading, or distribution of this book via the Internet is permissible.

The author, writers, and publisher have made every effort to include accurate information and website addresses in this work at the time of publication, and assume no responsibility for changes, omissions, inaccuracies, or errors that occur before or after publication. The publisher does not endorse or assume responsibility for information, author and writer websites, or third-party websites, or their content.

Library of Congress Control Number: 2014937298
Start Right Marketing: The Business of Making an Impact

1. Marketing 2. Business

ISBN-10:194027804X
ISBN-13:978-1-940278-04-9

Marketing/Business
Printed in the United States of America.

Cover Images:
Andreas Hartung | 31380911 | Dreamstime
Eti Swinford | 4137821 | Dreamstime

For more information, or to order bulk copies of this book for events, seminars, conferences, or training, please contact SplendorPublishing.com.

Dedication

I would like to dedicate this book to those who are brave enough to step up, take risk, and share their business and life success and—atheir failures—so others can follow, relate, know what to avoid, and learn what to apply for their own growth.

In addition, I'd like to thank those who support them—and of course me—so we can lead, participate, and connect with amazing people, just like you. When we have support from family, friends, associates, mentors, coaches, mastermind groups, and consultants, it gives us the luxury of time to do projects like this.

Enjoy the book and connect with each of us!

Tracy Repchuk,
International Bestselling Author and Speaker

Contents

Chapter 1
How to Shine Online and Reach Millions with Your Message
by Tracy Repchuk   1

Chapter 2
Speaking and Engaging Your Audience for the Ultimate Impact
by Jim Meskimen   17

Chapter 3
Mindset and Motivation—Find the Hero in You
by Fantastic Frank Johnson   27

Chapter 4
Three Secret Tricks to Get Unstuck and Unleash Your Wealth and Joy
by MarBeth Dunn   41

Chapter 5 How to Get a Product Name Loved by Millions Around the Globe—The 4 Attractions of a Winning Name
by Canon Wing   49

Chapter 6
7 Steps to Emails that Make Friends and Influence People
by Michele Camacho   63

Chapter 7
The Health of Your Business
by Susie Garcia, RDN   79

Chapter 8
Connecting Your Business for Global Impact
by Alberto Liberal   **95**

Chapter 9
Networking Mastery
by Sam Rafoss, RHN   **111**

Chapter 10   Increase Your Reach through Internet Radio,
Web TV, and Live Events
by Nadine Lajoie   **121**

Chapter 11
Growing Your Influence and Impact to Epidemic Levels
by Teresa de Grosbois   **131**

Chapter 12   Two Big Bangs for Your Influence-Marketing
Buck: Publish a Book and a Digital Magazine
by Margo DeGange   **149**

Chapter 1

How to Shine Online and Reach Millions with Your Message
by Tracy Repchuk

I'll never forget back in 1994 when I walked into a book store in Toronto Canada, and they had a full wall with books about the Internet. With hundreds of books about HTML, Java, SEO, protocols, languages—I was like a kid in a candy store. I was already in the technology field, so this was right up my alley. I spent $600 that day on books (this was pre Amazon days), and took my treasures home. Immediately I started to investigate HTML. I learned the language so I could develop websites, and I created my first site for my software company called Bravo Software Group (http://www.bravosw.com). We were among the first 100,000 websites to be online. After almost thirty years now in technology, my experiences range from integrating handhelds and software products, to accounting systems with companies such as Walmart, JC Penney, Home Depot, and many more, to developing software for Playmobil, governments, lottery corporations and banks. In 2007 I shifted our efforts to the marketing side of the Internet, and quickly realized the formula for rising above the noise and being deemed an expert in your industry.

From the technical world of programming, to becoming a bestselling author, to international speaker and motivator in over thirty countries around the world, and now a TV regular for business, I made it my mission to guide you along the best steps for where you are, and where you want to be, so you can dominate your market.

Here I present you with an overview of the five steps, which include:

Step 1—Your Branded Website

Step 2—The Internet Foundation

Step 3—Traffic and Leads: the Life of Your Business

Step 4—Business-Critical Social Media Sites

Step 5—Putting it All Together

Step 1—Your Branded Website

I am still in shock when I encounter businesses that don't have a website, because for the last ten years, the Internet has been the dominant partner for marketing your services. I think many businesses in 2009 discovered this too late when they had no customers, no money, and they were struggling or declaring bankruptcy. The Internet is not something that can be ignored, and using it needs to become a dominant strategy—in fact it should have its own marketing plan, in addition to your master marketing plan. (Many companies don't have either, but that is another story.)

Now with teens making millions with Internet apps and niche sites, the baby boomer generation is sitting paralyzed as to what to do next. In today's business environment, it's harder and harder to stay ahead if you are not in touch with your target market.

Most corporate or business sites are a brochure of what a company offers, and many are so vague and ambiguous in what they deliver, that even if they managed to get eyeballs to look, visitors would likely leave scratching their heads.

The good news is, it's not too late to jump in with both feet and get everything corrected and back on track.

Here are the top elements your branded site should include:

- A banner that clearly represents what you do, with your unique selling proposition (USP)

- Simple to follow options along the top

- A sidebar with easy links to key elements you offer

- A blog integrated to leverage SEO with Google

- Search Engine Optimization (SEO)

- Your social media links—easily available and integrated

- Images and text that directly target your market demographics

- What's in it for the potential customer right on the front page

The unique selling proposition (USP) normally consists of between three and ten words that describe the most powerful benefits you offer your customers and what sets you apart.

Here are examples of some that we have in various campaigns:

"We Take the Scary Out of Internet Marketing and Do it For You!"

"We Put the Marketing Into Your Internet Plan."

"Fully Branded End-to-End Website Presence in Under 60 days!"

Your USP is the force that drives your business and success. It can also be used as a "branding" tool that deploys strategy through your marketing. This allows you to build a lasting reputation while you're making sales. The ultimate goal of your USP and marketing is to have people instantly understand what you do, who you target, and how you can help them.

For an example of some sites that get the message across check out:

http://www.TracyRepchuk.com

http://www.InnerSurf.com

Knowing your unique selling proposition will not only save you on costly marketing mistakes but it can also turn your business around to make it more profitable very quickly.

Then it's not over. That was STEP 1. You still have a lot of work ahead of you, because the days of surviving on just one website are gone, and it's time to make list building, customer attraction, and social media a part of your marketing model.

Step 2—The Internet Foundation

The reason many companies are struggling today, is because their marketing plans have not included the web/Internet or a way to raise their profile immediately above the competition. Branding and Positioning have not been taken into account.

To beat the competition, your website must be found in spite of all the other options out there. That means a new approach to where you spend your advertising dollars, and a marketing plan that focuses on what the Internet can do for you.

If your target market doesn't "get" what makes your business and services unique from your competitors, you'll lose a lot of business and possibly not even know why. Swimming in the "sea of sameness" with your marketing is a very vulnerable place to be. Chances are it is a place of struggle and frustration, and if your customers continue to not be able to find you—or understand what you do—they will end up doing business with your competition.

The order of importance is critical here:

1. Your vision

2. Brand

3. Landing page

4. Emails

5. SEO

6. Social media

7. Corporate/branded site sales page

8. Traffic

9. Sales page—product highlight pages

That is what will equal success!

Most companies *only* have a business website. If that is the case for your business, you only have one-half of the websites required. Given the possible investment you may have done on your corporate site, that statement might seem a bit upsetting right now. I can guarantee though, that a few additional sites will create that autopilot mechanism you have dreamed of when it comes to attracting clients, closing deals, and crushing your competition!

I'm going to focus on the biggest breakthrough you can add to your online marketing . . . *your landing page*!

Your landing page is a capture page for collecting names and email addresses. This page will become your best friend because the modern way to build a client list is done *online*, with a landing page. This page has one purpose and that is to get the name and email address off the visitor so you can start a relationship with them, and in exchange you will give them an immediate gift. This allows you to build a list of people who know you, like you, trust you, and buy from you.

Step 3—Traffic and Leads: the Life of Your Business

Traffic is the lifeblood for everything you do. Without it, the phones don't ring, your websites have no activity, and customers don't find out—which means your message doesn't get out. There are many methods to getting traffic and attention to your business. I will focus on some of the top strategies here.

If you have already been in business, the first step is to leverage your existing clients, get referrals from them, reinvigorate your past clients, and—where the problem for many lies—get future clients. The fastest most targeted way is to dominate the Internet for your keywords.

SEO (Search Engine Optimization) Strategies

The key to what you do online is to attract the attention of Google. That's because Google rules where you appear in the search engines. Unless someone is specifically looking for you, you'll *need* search engine ranking. So, ensure that when you create a blog post, an article, a press release, a landing page, a sales page, a corporate site, etc., you know what your keywords are and you use them effectively. Before you can optimize your searches though, you have to know what your keywords are: you must find the words your customers are using to search for you, and the words your competition is using to beat you out, and use those words!

Articles and Press Releases

So why should you create articles and press releases, especially if you think you have nothing to talk about or nothing to say? The reason is because it's not about you. It is about putting out something that has your keywords in it, and driving them back to your site.

Why do it on an article or press release site? Because they have what is called a "high page rank." That means Google really respects these sites, and if you are on them, your importance goes up. They see you have a link, and they increase the value of your site. This is using leverage.

The key to creating traffic is to work it every day. This is the lifeblood of your company, and if ignored, it will lead to a very quiet office, no sales, no customers, and you scrambling to figure out what went wrong.

So create a calendar and put something in it every day, with the goal of the day, the keyword you want to leverage, the call-to-action, and the hopeful outcome. This is the only way you can understand what is working in your business.

Step 4—Business-Critical Social Media Sites

One of the most extensive changes for business today is the explosion of social media. Most people jump into social media—Facebook, YouTube, Twitter, LinkedIn, Google+, etc.—with no idea of what they are doing. Then two things happen:

1. You think social media is a waste of time.

2. You *are* wasting your time.

Social media is an integrated structure and part of your Internet marketing and branding *plan*. It is also purpose-driven, which means every tweet, post, and connection has a premeditated goal. The goal can be:

- More customers

- More sales

- Survey

- Engage

- Invite to an event

The goal can be anything, as long as it is not vague, useless, wastes your and their time, or has no value to the advancement of your goal.

With the social media onslaught, many companies are either ignoring social media hoping it will go away, or waiting until it becomes easier. The issue is, it is *not* going away, and your competition is probably already there. Here is a summary of the social media sites on which you should show up:

1. Facebook Fan Page

Make this your company name if you have a business, or your personal name if you are an author or speaker and you *are* the brand. If you don't already have a Facebook account, know this is now the largest social media platform with nearly a billion members globally, so become a member, it's easy and free. Set up professional Facebook "Pages" for both yourself and your business. If you don't know how to create your Facebook pages, make sure you get help from a professional who is up-to-date with the latest information, as social media platforms are dynamic and are always changing! The successful action is to start posting to your Facebook pages on a daily basis.

http://www.Facebook.com/TracyRepchukFan

2. LinkedIn

LinkedIn is for professionals and is designed to connect you with peers and opportunities for cross marketing, promotions, networking, and clients. LinkedIn is the next most important place to have your professional profile listed. There are a lot of ways you can use LinkedIn to connect with other professionals, generate leads in your ideal target market (assuming it's not outside of the LinkedIn demographic range), and run video and event promotions. When setting up your profile, make sure you get professional assistance to get the maximum advantage for your efforts and expert positioning.

> http://www.LinkedIn.com/in/TracyRepchuk

3. Twitter

Because you can integrate Twitter to send your blog posts and your Facebook posts automatically, this is a good tool to use because it is the fastest list building option I have found. It is worth establishing your company name on Twitter as well. In this social media platform you have two objectives:

> 1. Tease them with a message within the 140 character limit and get them to take the next action.

> 2. Drive them to your landing page and build your database.

> http://www.Twitter.com/TracyRepchuk

4. YouTube

Create videos that educate others about your products and services, promote and gather testimonials, and make each video have one goal—whatever that may be. *Always* have a call-to-action as the last slide, such as find out more about product X at product X page (be specific, not general). Or drive people to your landing page and build your list. That is always time well spent. YouTube is now the second most popular search engine after Google, and video marketing is still one of the most under-utilized and highest potential impact ways to get attention today. Set up a professional YouTube channel for yourself and secure the channel for each of your books. Videos on YouTube can then be easily played on your website with a simple embed code provided by YouTube.

http://www.YouTube.com/tracyrepchuk

5. Google +

Google + should be a part of your overall Google positioning simply because of the power they hold. All the Google products, including YouTube that is owned by Google, are connected and support each other. Google plus is the only social media platform that indexes on Google. So if you have a Gmail account or YouTube account you will already have a Google+ presence. You should set this up professionally and connect with your existing community by adding them to your circles, at the very least, as all of this will assist with your overall social media and search engine clout.

https://plus.google.com/u/0/+TracyRepchukTV

No matter who your ideal clients and target audience are, it's likely that they are on one form of social media or another.

Step 5—Putting it All Together

Now, if you are hiring someone like me to put this together for you, that's a very smart decision. That's because you are good at what you do, and I'm good at taking an author, speaker, coach, artist, or any business online.

Going online isn't just about having a website; it's having a brand, message, and signature product that is streamlined to target a market, and create a cohesive strategy that produces results.

If for budget reasons you absolutely have to do it yourself, then do one step at a time, and get that stable. Then add the next step, and always keep moving. If you get stuck, get unstuck. Do whatever it takes because if your websites aren't helping you, they're hurting you.

If you look at the historical models of business, we averaged $3000 per month for yellow page advertising. I did five trade shows a year at a cost ranging from $8000 - $18,000 per show. We have become so spoiled at the low operating cost of a business, that marketing budgets are being forgotten. We operate on a laptop, from the home, with a few domains, and a cell phone. It's definitely a brilliant opportunity to be able to become an entrepreneur, but remember, you are running a business that will take fuel, and your website and a marketing budget is that fuel.

I'll see you on the other side. It's my mission to help you get your message out there, and it's your goal to do it fast because money loves speed!

Check out how I can help you get started with *all* you need for your social media, unique selling proposition, full website review, your landing page, a domain name, and a free gift guide title: head over to http://www.OnlineClarityCleanse.com

Tracy's Special Offer:

Give yourself the gift of clarity!

Schedule your Online Clarity Cleanse and also receive this **Fast Action Bonus**: 3 Days of Live Training with Tracy and Tracy's online training, The Science of Social Media, at:

http://www.OnlineClarityCleanse.com

About Tracy Repchuk

Tracy Repchuk is an online marketing, social media, and business strategist, and a speaker. She is an international best-selling author, and has been an award-winning entrepreneur since 1985. She has helped thousands of clients get their messages out around the world.

Tracy is an internationally acclaimed speaker and motivator in over 35 countries. She keeps audiences engaged with her ability to break down complex concepts and turn them into formula-based success.

Tracy started her first software business at the age of nineteen, which still supports Fortune 100 companies. She has been nominated for awards such as "Entrepreneur of the Year," "Chamber of Commerce Business Woman of the Year," "Coach of the Year," and *Stevie Awards* for "Business Mentor of the Year." She has received "Provincial Volunteer" and software development awards, and has appeared in the *International Who's Who* in seven categories.

Tracy graduated in Business Computer Systems, and went on to receive a Certified Management Accountants designation. In 2007, she won "New Internet Marketing Success of the Year" from the World Internet Summit, and catapulted into success with her best-selling book, as well as through her speaking engagements and extensive Internet experience in web development, software integration, and marketing since 1994.

Tracy specializes in online marketing campaigns that build a cohesive corporate or personal brand, using an integrated web strategy that helps you attract more leads, get more clients, and make more money. Her solutions are done with marketing and results in mind. In addition, she has appeared as a technology specialist in national TV segments with *ABC7, San Diego Living, Good Morning New Mexico, CNBC, 4 Your Money, Report on Business, HGTV, FOX, CTV, CBS, NBC, KMIR, Life Love's Shopping, Daytime, Fox 5 Las Vegas, New Mexico Style, Vegas Inc, The CW, USA Today, Forbes, MSN Money, King5, CW,* and over fifty publications, newspapers, and magazines, plus two motivational movies.

Grab a free gift from Tracy, at:
http://www.FastActionResults.com

Chapter 2

Speaking and Engaging Your Audience for the Ultimate Impact
by Jim Meskimen

As an impressionist/comedian, spokesman, and presenter for almost thirty years, I've faced audiences of all types and sizes, sometimes with carefully worked out material, sometimes with only a general outline of points to be addressed, and sometimes with no preparation at all.

Audiences have taught me a lot, and continue to teach me with every presentation I give. It's not always a comfortable lesson, but eventually you learn how to deal with audiences and how to communicate without falling to pieces, becoming drenched in flop sweat, or worst of all, failing to get the message across.

Connecting with the group in front of you is a key thing on which to concentrate. If you don't connect, you can't expect to engage and achieve your goal of getting an idea across. Like those annoying calls you get from "boiler room" telemarketers, who begin to rattle off their spiel without asking if you are even vaguely interested in their offer, your speech risks earning a "hang-up" unless you establish a willingness to engage in the first place.

It's a funny thing that my best results have often been accompanied by the least amount of carefully worked out material; the times I improvised consistently yielded better presentations with more engagement. I wondered about that, about why that should be.

Of course, I'm very comfortable with improv, having done thousands of improvised shows in New York and L.A. with a variety of different groups, and I've made up scenes and even songs on television on episodes of *Whose Line is it, Anyway?*, *World Cup Comedy*, *America's Got Talent*, and others.

I've even experienced extremes of both bad and good audience reactions: receiving a standing ovation at Radio City Music Hall in New York while I was a semifinalist on *America's Got Talent*, and literally having rotting vegetables flung at me in a college stage production in Santa Cruz. All other reactions have fallen somewhere in between those events.

But even if you are not a seasoned veteran of the improv stage, or have never dodged a tomato hurled in anger, there is a point about engagement with an audience that can be practiced by anyone.

The main point is to address the audience in front of you right *now*, instead of some fancied, generalized crowd. The reason improv works so well for a live audience has to do with the immediacy of the specific group one is in front of; there is an inherent shared connection there and a dialogue in real time.

When you are nervous or anxious about addressing a group, you are anticipating the reaction of a presumably hostile or unsympathetic collection of people. This prediction can easily become a self-fulfilling prophecy, as anyone who has watched their own presentation spiral out of control can testify.

But how does one prepare remarks in sufficient detail and in a coherent way, and still remain fluid enough to respond to and influence the exact audience one is speaking to, so as to achieve the maximum result?

Speaking and Engaging Your Audience for the Ultimate Impact

The key is in preparation, then practice, then in tossing it all away and speaking directly to the group one is in front of, in that moment.

I recall being in an audience listening to two speakers at a symposium, both of whom were well-regarded and one of whom was rather famous. One spoke extemporaneously, and from the heart, while the more famous one strolled around giving a canned talk that he had delivered so many times before, he might have been doing it with his mind totally occupied with other things. I can't remember a single thing that famous speaker said, but more than twenty years later, I can recall specific points made by the first guy who was personally invested in what he was telling us.

I'm sure you've had similar experiences listening to people give talks; the ones you remember and carry with you were so interested in sharing their thoughts with the people in front of them that they had a lasting impact.

So, how do you do that with your speeches, so that you aren't forgotten? Here are some tips I've picked up along my way.

Tip #1—Use Humor

When you speak to any size crowd, humor is a key tool. You actually don't need to be a stand-up comedian, and frankly you are better off *not* trying to bully people into laughing at some set routine. As with the "famous speaker" above, if you rely on canned materiel to do all your heavy lifting, and never invest yourself in the existing mood of your current audience, you can wave your chances at engagement bye-bye.

You use humor for a very good reason: to begin to foster that most useful of things when dealing with groups—*agreement*.

Simply put, when you get a laugh, that's a sign they agree with what you said. It's a survey you conduct in the midst of giving your speech. You suggest something's "funny" (or wrong, disagreeable, out of place, ridiculous) and they laugh to tell you, "*Yeah, I think so too.*" "*Agreed.*"

Of course, you first have to work out what they might agree to. We've all seen bad comics—on stage or at the water cooler—who put out observations that don't "agree" with us because of bad taste or ignorance. We don't laugh; we walk away. No laugh = *no agreement.* (No invitation to do stand—up at the company party, either.)

Then there is the "stale joke" that is so old, you just can't be bothered to agree with it anymore. Only very polite audiences will chuckle at the old "tried and true" humorous asides, and then when you ask them to do something tangible, they may just as politely back down and leave you standing alone with your premise.

Generally, conferences and business meetings are about getting, fostering, or establishing agreement; agreement about strategy, goals, terms, direction, etc.; agreement on how tough things are, and how dedicated and focused teams will have to be to succeed.

Agreement is actually a kind of flow: it builds, and if you get enough of it going, you can accomplish miracles. At first, you just need to get that flow going, and by degrees, get that trickle of agreement to cut its way into a wider and wider channel.

You can more easily start the flow of agreement on complex, serious things by starting with simple, low-stakes things... like casual, humorous observations.

The sooner you get that flow of agreement going, and then keep it going by whatever shifts, the sooner you will get agreement on the bigger topics you want your group to embrace, and the sooner you will get them into action.

If you neglect to obtain agreement, you can talk until your face turns magenta, and still be ineffective. It's not about how long, how loud, how cleverly, or how professionally you speak, it's about what you say that they *agree* with and will be willing to act on.

Humor can help you get started, and can also help over the rough patches along the way, when agreement—like the NASDAQ—takes an unanticipated dip.

So, where could laughter help in your presentation? You can feel it, whenever you are addressing the crowd and *agreement* starts to evaporate. Use humor to get it back again.

Tip #2—Consider Clarity and Simplicity

Clarity and simplicity are two virtues you should also keep in mind when preparing a speech. It may seem very obvious, but if you aren't clear about what you are talking about, your audience isn't going to absorb your message.

You may have a ton of facts to disgorge about your field of expertise, and lots and lots of information to share, but the *purpose* of why you are speaking to them and the broad strokes of what you want them to walk away with should be top of mind with you before you begin. All the minor points, minutiae, and details can be jettisoned, but the important overall message must never be left behind. A good thing to consider is what would your speech contain if it was distilled into one or two short statements? It's a good habit to ask yourself before you address a group, *"What do I want them to get out of my talk? If they remember* **nothing** *else, what should the take-away be?"*

A side benefit of this might be that you don't really need to talk for two hours; thirty minutes might be plenty. Cut out everything that doesn't contribute to your message. You shouldn't have to pad the speech just to fill time. Very few things in life require a filibuster. The Gettysburg Address was delivered in under three minutes.

Mastering your message means knowing it, being willing to simplify it to make it assimilable, and sacrificing all else in the service of being understood.

Tip #3—Offer a Unique Viewpoint

Shock comedians use graphic language to make an impact and get an audience to react, usually with uncomfortable laughter. Comedian Lenny Bruce became famous for using "outrageous" language that today seems mild and naive compared to contemporary stand-ups. Over time, the shock value of certain words and situations is so overused, they no longer produce any impact; like the 10,000th punch to the skull of a prizefighter, they are relatively unfelt.

If you review the speakers who have had an impact on you in the past, what did they do to produce that effect? Did they offer a unique viewpoint? Did they relate a story you found compelling? Did they reveal something about themselves that was daring, or unexpected, or inspiring?

Tip #4—Make an Impact

All the prior points I've mentioned play a part here; if you have mastered your message, distilling it to its basics, spoken from the heart and perhaps made them laugh a bit along the way, you have a good chance of making an impact.

Speaking and Engaging Your Audience for the Ultimate Impact

You making an impact is what people are there for, actually. They *want* to be impacted upon. They have a hunch *you* might be the one to do it, so they are lending you some of their valuable attention. The vast majority of people going to a football game want to see something *happen*. They aren't there just to watch the huddles.

To have an impact, you have to be willing to have your audience *be* impacted upon. Don't withdraw, or apologize, or understate. Let 'em have it! If there are uncomfortable truths to utter, don't sugarcoat them. Let that impact your listeners. If there is a solution, don't omit to let *that* hit them between the eyes just as hard.

Look at your audience when you say key things. If you have to read it first off the page or the teleprompter, fine. But then look at them and repeat it. Be willing to be impactful.

By the way, what do you reckon has the *most* power to cut through the clutter and noise and have an impact? *Truth!* What is the truest thing in your presentation? Define *that*, and you have the straightest and sharpest arrow in your quiver. But first, be *willing* to have an impact on others. That's what they are waiting for, actually!

Audience Comfort

Lastly, don't overstay your welcome. Never say in fifty words what you can say in ten.

Everyone, generally speaking, has a rear end. All rear ends, regardless of how soft the chair, get uncomfortable sooner or later. Make sure you keep part of your attention on the comfort/exhaustion level of your audience, and cut to the final summation the minute you detect the slumping, shifting, and other indications of impending slumber that spell "audience disengagement." You may have made your point long before, and now over-saturation has made them paralyzed and limp. Less *is* more.

Thanks for reading, and good luck in your next presentation!

Jim's Special Offer:

To keep in touch with Jim's appearances and opportunities, and get his free guide,
7 Ways to Engage an Audience and Master Your Message
visit:
http://www.TopComedianSpeaker.com

About Jim Meskimen

As a professional actor for thirty years, Jim Meskimen has appeared in the films *Apollo 13*, *The Grinch*, Frost/Nixon, *The Punisher*, Not Forgotten, *There Will Be Blood*, and many others. Some of Jim's TV credits include *Friends*, *Whose Line is it, Anyway?*, *Fresh Prince of Bel Air*, *Castle*, *Lie to Me*, and *Parks & Recreation*.

In the 1980s and 1990s, Jim had a thriving career as a man-on-the-street interviewer for improvised TV and radio campaigns for grocery stores, bank cards, coffee makers, and a host of other clients who won awards for several major advertising agencies.

As an impressionist, Jim's impressions of political figures in the 2004 election were showcased in animated cartoons by Jibjab that were among the most popular items on the Internet. His viral video, *Shakespeare in Celebrity Voices*, topped nearly one million views, and his subsequent impressions videos have cemented him as a major YouTube talent. *The Australian Today Show* dubbed him, "The World's Greatest Impressionist."

Meskimen lives in Los Angeles with his wife, actress and founder of The Acting Center school, Tamra Meskimen. His daughter, Taylor, is also a performer, and his mother is actress Marion Ross, who was Emmy and Golden Globe nominated for her work on *Happy Days* (as Richie's mom) and *Brooklyn Bridge*.

Catch Jim Meskimen in JIMPRESSIONS, his hilarious one-man show featuring dozens of incredible celebrity impressions. Filmed live at the historic Capitol Theater in Clearwater, Florida, JIMPRESSIONS is two full acts of improvisation, stories, and celebrity voices, over 75 different impressions that will make your jaw drop in amazement (order your DVD here: http://appliedsilliness.com/jimpressionsdvd.html).

Jim currently stars in *The Impression Guys*, a web series about the life of a couple of impressionists who yearn to be taken seriously as actors, on the *SoulPancake* channel on https://www.youtube.com/user/soulpancake.

To find out more about Jim, visit: http://www.JimMeskimen.com

Chapter 3

Mindset and Motivation— Find the Hero in You
by Fantastic Frank Johnson

My most vivid memory from Sunday, January 4, 1981, is my heart-wrenching conclusion *"I am going to die."* Elsewhere on that record cold minus-ten degree day in Rochester, NY, teeth were chattering and car engines were grinding; but from where I lay, in the basement office of a building raging with fire, it was "hot as a pistol." Heat and dense smoke almost aborted my rescue. *"It took a while for us to find him"* said Fire Chief Ippolito to reporters.

Days later, I passed through the semi-death of a coma and awakened in what doctors declared to be a "medical miracle." Everything was a blur. Unable to walk, talk, or even think straight, I felt cursed. At 31 years old, the fire bestowed me with a permanent traumatic brain injury (TBI), and there was no going back. Engineering career, bar and restaurant business, home, relationships of all kinds, were effectively burnt in the fire.

That was over thirty years ago and back then, not as much was known about the brain. The term "traumatic brain injury" or "TBI" wasn't even used. No one understood my condition, and after intensive physical rehabilitation, I was sent home from the hospital to cope on my own with the mental and emotional aspect of my injuries. Holes in memory, and intensified liabilities, unraveled daily progress. For about twenty years TBI's "silent epidemic" had me in its clutches.

Then, remarkably, I was blessed with a number of significant breakthroughs. The tables were turned; amidst the difficulty, a diamond in the rough came to light when the TBI shifted my personality in a positive way. Compassion, a sense of connectedness, and true caring for others entered my heart when I wasn't looking. Ever since, an overwhelming passion to help others overcome challenges directs my life, from when I awake in the morning, to when I retire at night.

So victorious was I, so elated to shed the identity of a "disabled" victim and re-enter life as "Differently-Abled," that I took on the "Fantastic Frank" persona. The "FF" emblem, on the chest of my super hero costume, inspires others that no matter how bad things may seem, no matter how great the challenge, you can make the choice to persevere, to love, and to be happy.

Dedicated to inspiring millions, I use every means I can to connect with others, from creating a comic book, writing the book "*From Flawed to Fantastic*," appearing on stages and TV stations all across the country, co-writing a song written called "*Hero in You*," to hosting a weekly BlogTalkRadio show.

My gift to you, dear reader, are my *7 Motivational Secrets to Excel Every Day*. They are universal ideas that will lift you up, regardless of your degree of "ability," economic status, education, race, gender, or nationality. They include:

Secret #1—Words Have Power

Secret #2—Find Gratitude and Abundance in Your Life

Secret #3—Inventory Your Life from the Center to Create a More Powerful One

Secret #4—What You Want with All Your Heart *Can* Come True

Secret #5—Use the Law of Attraction to Change Your Life

Secret #6—Passion is More Powerful than Fear

Secret #7—Use Affirmations to Propel Your Life Forward

"People with disabilities constitute the nation's largest minority group, the single largest minority group seeking employment in today's marketplace, and the only group any of us can become a member of at any time. Of the 69.6 million families in the United States, more than 20 million have at least one family member with a disability."
–Maryland Department of Disabilities,
www.mdod.maryland.gov

Secret #1—Words Have Power

"Over 77 percent of the population has some sort of label that puts you at a disability in your job, your career and in life!" –Fantastic Frank Johnson

Do not underestimate the power of words. If you repeatedly refer to yourself as "disabled," you are locking yourself into a box of "disability." This becomes your identity; in your own eyes, and the eyes of others. To break out of this box, what I do is call myself "differently-abled," or "Fantastic Frank." When you refer to yourself as "differently-abled," the person with whom you are speaking is less likely to put you in the "disabled" box. "Dis-abled" indicates not being "able," and stops there. "Differently—abled" goes straight to being "able" in a different way.

Another way to reinforce your new self-concept is to say that you've gone *From Flawed to Fantastic*, which is the title of a book I wrote, with detailed steps on how to do just that.

Now, take this a step further, and realize you are a super hero. Super heroes such as Superman, the Flash, the Incredible Hulk, Spider-Man, and the Fantastic Four, were all endowed with super powers when something traumatic happened to them.

For example, Spider-Man was bitten by a radioactive spider. In an "ah ha moment," I realized that, the life-changing trauma—of getting a TBI and losing the "life" I had known—gave me the "power" to deeply touch and inspire others as a motivational speaker. Although not as flashy as the heroes of my youth, with this "power" of inspiring others, I have been granted my childhood wish of growing up and becoming a super hero.

How about you? The fact that you are here right now, receiving this message, means your mission—or your purpose on Earth—has not yet been fulfilled, because you are still here. Whatever your story is, whatever challenges you have to overcome, there is something unique to you; something wonderful and powerful. I know this because this is true of everyone. It just needs to be recognized and tapped into.

Celebrate life by acknowledging the super and heroic things you have been empowered to do. Give thanks for your "powers," and use them for good. Share your super hero story with someone; your spouse, kids, friends... if you say you have no one, share it with me!

Secret #2—Find Gratitude and Abundance in Your Life

The secret to having peace in your heart is that you have to be grateful for everything you have, whether or not you initially perceive it as "good" or "bad." This is true gratitude.

The tide of true gratitude quickly flows into abundance. By "abundance" I mean having a large amount of something (not necessarily material wealth and the power that comes with it). Abundance goes beyond the gratitude for your own individual life, to the knowledge that what you do makes a difference in other people's lives. How do I know this?

Through my life's journey, I have come to realize that true abundance is not a place in which we live, nor is it defined by how much money we have. It is defined by how much love or positive energy we share with anyone, which touches countless other lives; much like the ripple effect seen when pebbles are cast into water.

When you can give of yourself, when you give love, you will always have ample abundance. Sharing your story helps others live fuller lives. You can even do TV segments across America to spread your message, as I have. To get ideas on how you can do this, too, see my media page:

http://www.fantasticfrankjohnson.com/media

Secret #3—Inventory Your Life from the Center to Create a More Powerful One

Now that you recognize you are a differently-abled super hero, and that you are full of gratitude, love, and abundance, it is time to take an inventory of your life; of where it is now versus the vision of what it can be. Life can be pictured as a spider web; everything is interconnected, with a very clear center. What is your life about—what's your "Web"? If you're not sure, start by finding the center; in other words, what you focus on the most.

- What are most of your thoughts about?
- How do you spend most of your time?
- What is most important to you?
- Do you spend time on your goals and dreams?
- How do you prioritize your time and resources?
- Who do you live with, listen to, trust, and have association with?
- Who lifts you up, and who drags you down?

All the things in your inventory are at the center of your web of life. Now take note of how the focus at the center affects everything else in your life, which is the rest of the web.

Do you like what you see, or do you want a different, more powerful life? For example, is money the focus of your life, when you'd prefer your life to be focused on your spirituality? Are you spending all your time in superficial activities that drain your energy and steal your dreams?

Have you noticed how quickly a spider can build a web? With laser sharp focus, your life can change just as fast. It all starts at the center.

Take the time to inventory your life, as one of the first steps in creating another, more powerful life. Along the way, become friends with people who support the direction in which you want to go, and who inspire you to get there. For starters, you can connect with *me* on Facebook:

http://www.Facebook.com/Fantasticfrank1

Secret #4—What You Want with All Your Heart *Can* Come True

What is the thing you most desire, and have told yourself you can never have?

- Do you have no legs and want to run?
- Do you have no voice and wish to speak?
- Do you live in isolation and crave intimacy?

To change your life, you must dare to believe that what you want with all of your heart can and will happen. You must also accept that the details of how this is accomplished may be different than what you hoped. For example, accept that your missing legs will not grow back again as the legs you had, while being open and grateful to "walking" again by other means.

The key is that when you get in touch with what you want with all your heart, and equally believe it will come to be, you give it the means to happen. Set the intention that what you want with all your heart will happen. Then let go of the attachment to its outcome. In particular, don't put a time limit on the actualization of the outcome (this may be the hardest part of all). If you do, and it doesn't happen by the time you wanted to, you may give up in despair. For me, it took about twenty years. Be grateful for whatever or whenever the results show up, without being surprised when you indeed get whatever it is you want or need.

For years I lived in isolation because I was embarrassed of my voice challenge. Today, I use my voice to inspire others, and people seek me out to motivate their teams. See more at:

http://www.fantasticfrankjohnson.com/speaker

Secret #5—Use the Law of Attraction to Change Your Life

You may be wondering how you are going to bring about a new life, when you don't even know where to begin, what steps to take, who to turn to, etc. The secret is, you don't have to know the details. Simply use the law of attraction. In its basic form, the law of attraction means that you attract to yourself whatever you focus on the most.

The law is occurring, whether or not you are conscious of it, just like gravity. For example, when you buy a car, you start seeing the same model and color car wherever you go.

That is because you had just put a great deal of attention on it. On a larger scale, if your tendency is to focus on stumbling blocks, you will continuously be stopped in your tracks by obstacles. On the other hand, if your tendency is to focus on opportunities, then you will have a knack for finding just what you need to break through to the next level.

To see that this is true, look back on your own life. Connect the dots to where your life is now, by backtracking significant past events. Where was your focus at each pivotal moment? Remember, *you get what you focus on.*

Armed with this knowledge, you can make better choices about your future. Use the law of attraction by:

◉ Being grateful that the universe is answering your requests.

◉ Being clear about your passion and focusing on it.

◉ Regularly visualizing your new life with strong emotional attachment.

◉ Acting on opportunities that are aligned with your vision.

◉ Persisting in being focused, while giving what you are attracting the time it needs to appear.

◉ Being grateful to receive the gifts, however they show up, which may not be as you had imagined.

By using this concept, I've attracted amazing guests to be on my weekly BlogTalkRadio show. Listen in live, or to archived episodes, and be inspired to go from *Flawed to Fantastic*:

http://www.fantasticfrankjohnson.com/radio

Secret #6—Passion is More Powerful than Fear

The prospect of changing your life can be scary. What has been certain will become uncertain. The more you focus on the possibilities, the more hopeful you are. The more attached you are to the outcome, the greater the risk of being disappointed.

When fear appears, turn your attention to your passion, to your vision of your new powerful life, and to all the reasons why you want and need to change. If this is truly something you want with all your heart, your passion will overcome your fear.

The less you focus on fear, the more it will fade away. Focusing on your passion is the fundamental means to overcoming fear. Once you are solid in your passion, there are practical steps to take:

1. Write down your passion, with your reason for wanting a change, and your vision of your new life.

2. Get down to what your specific fear is: is it fear of public speaking, rejection, financial ruin, failure…?

3. Realize that there is a way out of your fear, by seeking out others who have gone beyond it. This help could be an organization, a mentor, an inspiring figure, etc.

Mindset and Motivation—Find the Hero in You

4. Model and learn from a person/organization with the correct knowledge and experiences relating to your specific fear. Apply this in your own life to the best of your abilities.

5. Whenever your fear returns, focus on your passion to overcome it. Be persistent.

For regular inspiration on overcoming fears and challenges of all kinds, read my blog:

http://www.fantasticfrankjohnson.com/blog

Secret #7—Use Affirmations to Propel Your Life Forward

Merely reading the steps in this chapter will accomplish nothing if you do not apply them in your life right away. Otherwise, your old habits and words will hold you back, and your inspiration will recede into the background.

A quick and simple way to take action now is with affirmations. Affirmations are powerful sentences that counter your old way of thinking, and redirect your life. They should state your vision in the present tense. Ideally, they should be said both aloud and silently, when you first wake up, throughout the day, and just before you go to sleep.

It is a good idea to write your affirmations on little cards and put them in various places; your pocket, the bathroom mirror, above the sink, in front of your computer, etc.

To get free *Affirmation Cards* based on these seven secrets, go to http://www.FFHero.com and sign up for the *Free Guide*, then click the *Special Bonus* link on the last page of the guide.

Start Right Marketing

Fantastic Frank's Special Offer:

Receive a free copy of Frank's,

7 Affirmation Cards

to print out and use to apply the 7 secrets, go to:

http://www.FFHero.com

About Fantastic Frank Johnson

Trapped in a Fire,
Carried out in a Body Bag,
Motivated to Inspire
Millions!

"I help business leaders inspire their teams to go beyond challenges so that personal breakthroughs translate into profits." - Fantastic Frank Johnson

Fantastic Frank is an award-winning dynamic motivational speaker and TV celebrity guest who inspires any audience to overcome and excel at life.

One day, while at the height of enjoying success, his life changed forever—he was trapped in a fire, carried out in a body bag, and incurred a traumatic brain injury. It was necessary for him to re-learn everything; including how to walk and talk.

The epitome of perseverance, he turned tragedy to triumph. Now, he appears across America in his signature super hero suit, motivated to inspire millions.

His book, *From Flawed to Fantastic*, takes people through a step-by-step process of life transformation. As an outstanding radio host, he provides hope and help on the *Traumatic Brain Injury (TBI) Network*. He also co-wrote the song *Hero In You*.

Recognized for his inspiring message, the story " Fantastic Frank" was published in *Chicken Soup for the Soul: Recovering from Traumatic Brain Injury*.

Fantastic Frank touches many people's lives. Let him touch yours! Get his free guide at:

    http://www.FFHero.com

To find out more about Fantastic Frank, or to book him to speak, visit:
http://www.FantasticFrankJohnson.com

Chapter 4

3 Secret Tricks to Get Unstuck and Unleash Your Wealth and Joy
by Marbeth Dunn

People come to me all the time because they're stuck. They are generally surprised to discover that the reasons they are unable to move forward stem from seemingly unrelated issues.

Let me ask you some important questions, so we can get to the root of what's holding you back from your greatest success:

- Are you feeling *stuck* and don't understand *why* your business isn't working?

- Are you afraid to take risks? Do you feel like you're in a downward spiral?

- Were you once successful, but now you can't seem to get ahead?

- Are you having trouble sleeping? Are your sleep patterns disrupted?

- Do you find yourself stressed, flying off the handle for no reason?

- Are you having a love affair with comfort food? Are you unhappy with your weight?

- Are you losing yourself in TV, shopping, or alcohol?

- Do you feel an ongoing sense of sadness or regret?

If you answered yes to any of these questions, the chances are good that you're being held back by at least one of the three major roadblocks to wealth and success: emotional barriers, unconscious thought patterns, and energetic issues. These issues can impact your life and your business in a multitude of ways, affecting your finances, business, self confidence, self image, relationships, and virtually every aspect of life.

Emotional Barriers

The most common barriers to wealth and joy are the emotionally charged after-effects of loss:

Loss of a loved one—Generally, people think of loss as the physical loss of a loved one through death, which can be one of the most devastating human experiences on this planet. Yet we lose loved ones in many ways . . . through divorce, abandonment, the ending of relationships, or relocation.

Loss of lifestyle—Lifestyles can change drastically when you lose a job or a home, or if you experience a health challenge.

"Hidden" Losses—These involve the not-so-easy-to-identify feelings that something is missing. Some examples of this include losing your power, self-esteem, or self-respect in a

relationship; or feeling that you've lost your sexiness, your health, or your youth. Other examples include missing your homeland, language, or culture of your childhood.

Why is it important to release these emotional barriers?

Your human body appears to be solid, yet science has shown that you are not a solid being at all. How can that be, you ask? "*I feel* solid!" It's because your body is composed of atoms, which are 99.99999999 percent empty space, with huge distances spanning the particles within. If you took all the matter within your body and compressed it, it would fit into the seed of an apple!

Remember that famous Einstein equation, $E=MC^2$? He proved that matter and energy are interchangeable. This means that you are potential energy!

Think of yourself as multidimensional patterns of light and information, with emotions and feelings flowing through you like clouds. When you suppress or hold onto old emotional baggage, the energy becomes trapped and blocks your energy flow. Since your outer world is reflective of your inner world, you may find your financial flow constricted, your relationships disrupted, or your world in a state of upheaval.

What do happiness and joy have to do with it?

Scientific research shows strong correlations between happiness and increased income and productivity. A recent study at the University of Western Sydney, Australia, shows happier people get more done at work and are paid more. Professor Satya Paul found that Australians who were most satisfied with life earned almost $1800 a year more than people at the bottom of the happiness scale.

Getting unstuck from your old baggage will make you feel lighter, happier, and free. This will, in turn, raise your energy level and your vibrational frequency. You will create the space to attract greater wealth, abundance, better relationships, and more vibrant health.

Creating positive thoughts can be very powerful. If however, you are stuck because of an old hurt or loss you haven't processed, or an old belief you haven't released, you may find yourself in conflict and resistance. Here are three things you can do right *now* to get unstuck and create miracles of joy and wealth:

1. Forgiveness is the Key to Happiness and Wealth!

I've always been inspired by Oprah. Not only has she overcome a rough, abusive childhood, and numerous career challenges and setbacks, she was fired as a television reporter for being "unfit for TV!" Yet by letting go and releasing the past, Oprah demonstrates the power of taking personal responsibility for her life. Had she held on to her grievances and played the victim, keeping herself small and diminished, she would never have risen to where she is today.

Forgiveness frees you to move forward. It is a shift in perception that allows you to release your anger, resentment, and emotional charge. It's not about the other person at all.

Forgiveness is the *complete letting go* of any emotional reactions or attachment associated with a situation where you felt victimized or wronged. It is not condoning what the other person did, nor do you need to allow them into your life again. True forgiveness is the release of the emotional *energy* associated with the person or event. Forgiveness doesn't mean you deny the other person's responsibility for hurting you. Not at all. You may still remember the act that hurt or offended you, but it will lose its charge. You can forgive the other person without minimizing or excusing what they did.

Holding a grievance shackles you to the other person, dragging him with you wherever you go. It holds *you* prisoner. Though you feel righteous, it can never bring you happiness.

Pick up a pen and hold it tightly in your hand, fingers facing down. Let the pen represent your anger and outrage. Now, open your hand and release the pen. That's how easy it can be to release your smoldering emotions and be free at last.

By forgiving the other person, you will feel expanded, free, and more joyful. You are reclaiming your personal power and releasing the energy of victim and perpetrator, thus allowing a brand new outcome. Forgiveness is a choice. Even though you may not feel ready to release your anger and pain, your willingness to do so will begin the process.

2. Let Yourself Off the Hook!

If you're like most people, you may find it easier to forgive others than to forgive yourself. Do you constantly beat yourself up for not measuring up to impossible standards? Does your inner critic chide you and remind you of all the reasons why you can't get what you want instead of encouraging you? Do you treat yourself like your best friend? Or do you sabotage yourself, constantly finding yet another fault?

It's time you stepped up to be the best friend you've always longed for, the one who . . . loves you unconditionally, is there to support you when you need it, is your strongest cheerleader and advocate, and will always encourage and guide you.

Sit quietly, take a couple of deep breaths, and ask yourself the following questions:

- ◎ What if I could be my very own best friend?

- What if I could focus on my best qualities?

- What if I could feel really good about myself?

- What would that feel like?

Don't answer the questions. Let them sit there and percolate. Open-ended questions are the key to transformation. They slide past your resistance and open you to new possibilities.

3. Hold the Focus!

Steven Spielberg always wanted to work in movies, yet he was rejected from University of Southern California School of Theater, Film, and Television three times. He held his focus. He knew what he wanted. After attending school in a different location, he dropped out to become a film director. Spielberg says, *"I don't dream at night, I dream at day, I dream all day; I'm dreaming for living."*

You can achieve your goals when you focus on what you want and give zero attention to what you don't want. Here's a great exercise to help you create what you desire: using crayons or markers, draw an image of your desired outcome for one specific thing. It doesn't matter whether you're artistic or not. This drawing is for your eyes only. Your drawing can be representational. It could be a stick figure. It simply must represent the essence of what you would like to experience. Be sure to include yourself in the drawing.

For example, if you would like a different environment for your career, one with a more natural setting, your drawing might show you with large windows overlooking a garden filled with flowers, birds, or butterflies. If you would like to create more money, you could draw yourself standing at an ATM, looking at the balance you desire (that you believe is possible).

The image you're drawing is a "billboard" for *your* eyes only. You're creating an advertising image for your most important client, *you*! It is essential that it excites you, and pulls you in. The very act of drawing it renders it yours. Keep your drawing handy and look at it often, knowing that what you desire is already yours.

The Joy to Abundance Strategist
Custom Created Solutions for a Life and Legacy of Health, Wealth and Happiness

MarBeth's Special Offer:

If you are serious about moving forward to create more wealth and joy in your life and business go to
http://YourJoyJourney.com

Get your free copy of MarBeth's

7 Steps to Get Unstuck and Unlock Your Joy

Then schedule a FREE one-on-one
Joy Readiness Consult with MarBeth

Take the brief assessment at **http://marbethdunn.com/survey**

About MarBeth Dunn

MarBeth Dunn, known as the Joy to Abundance Strategist and TV Happiness Coach, is an empath and intuitive, an author, international speaker, coach, mentor, and radio host.

If you are a heart-centered entrepreneur feeling unsure of your life's purpose, or stuck in your career, relationships, or finances, MarBeth can help.

MarBeth works with holistic entrepreneurs to remove *all* barriers to their success. She can help you confidently align with your purpose, joyfully accelerate your growth, and unleash your intuitive genius. Aligned with your *Soul's Purpose*, and free of the impediments to your life's expression, you cannot help but soar like an eagle, happy and free. MarBeth is the author of The *Ultimate Joy Strategy: 31 Days to Health, Wealth and Happiness*. Her inspiring work has been featured on FOX, NBC, CBS, The CW in San Diego, and WEYW 19, Key West, where she is a regular guest.

**To find out more about Marbeth, visit:
http://www.MarBethDunn.com**

Chapter 5

How to Get a Product Name Loved by Millions Around the Globe— The 4 Attractions of a Winning Name
by Canon Wing

Your name must be the greatest story ever told! Let me tell you a story about how a name can make or break your business. If you are ready to see it, you are about to gain a philosophy that you can use to enjoy material wealth, love, peace, health, spiritual enlightenment, and ultimately to recover from any ailment that keeps you small or stagnant. Ready? You are about to expose yourself to an influence that has been a universal truth for all of time, and once you truly see it, you will see where you abuse it, ignore it, or, throw it away, and also where you can reclaim it and empower it. It is my hope you will use it to enrich your life and those of everyone you love; which is to say absolutely everyone.

To begin our story: I am flying home to LA from a snowy family Christmas in New York. My boyfriend Omry is feeling faint and needs to be carried off the plane by the stewards and a few kind passengers. We get him to Cedars Sinai Hospital where a young ER doctor comes through the curtains to say, "*Oh dude, you got cancer.*"

I just faint, straight shot onto the linoleum floor. As we wheel his bed into the ICU, my boyfriend looks up at me and asks, *"Did I go through this life, invisible?"* I watch him go from being this gorgeous runway model, to a week later, an ashen skeleton in his hospital bed. I stay with him 24/7. We never see our apartments again. Sometimes I sleep on the floor outside the ICU, or sitting next to his bed. In the dead of night, his brain slips down into his throat, choking him from a stroke. I call the "Code Blue" as he speaks the final words *"I love you,"* as they wheel him into twelve hours of surgery. Later, the doctors called me outside his room. They surround me in their white coats and hand me his sentence. They name him paralyzed, blinded, epileptic, handicapped, and crippled for life. Has anyone ever named you less than—tried to make you invisible? Well, I told them *"No!"* They said, *"There is no medical evidence to the contrary."* I said, *"How can there be? You can not measure the will in another man's heart or the love in mine. Can you? You look at him. He's the Miracle Man and I forbid you to call him any other name, because you don't have any evidence to the contrary, do you?"* One of them shrugged, another nodded her head. *"Promise me you will not call him any other name than the Miracle Man."* They nodded, and I turned and ran back to my love—his face half paralyzed, so half smiling at me, unaware. I said, *"Baby, they said you're going to get it all back. You're the Miracle Man."*

    Two years later we danced the fox trot at our wedding like we were made of fire. I know there are people out there naming your dream "Impossible." I know it could disable you. It's not even something they are conscious of.

    I bet they're not trying to hurt you. They might be thinking they don't want to see you get hurt. They think they are helping you by naming you less than.

    The naysayers will come. But if you can see it, they don't come to beat you down, they come to give *you* the opportunity

How to Get a Product Name Loved by Millions Around the Globe

to build yourself up. Because it is vital to your greatness to get the naysayers out of your head, out of your heart, and out of your path.

I want you to see that your path is the path to helping others achieve their greatness. Your name is the first step and the most important step towards a greater future for them. And if you can name that greater future they will buy it.

I have been very fortunate and honored to name people's dreams into greatness for over two decades. And I know you are here right now reading these words because you're ready to let your greatness see the light of day. I truly know my story exists to help you find your way without having to experience what I did. Likewise, your story exists to help others more easily step into their greatness. I'm here to help you name it. Victor Hugo said, *"There is nothing more powerful than an idea whose time has come."* Has your time finally come?

A Great Name = Free Word-of-Mouth Advertising for Life

I am going to share with you the exact method I used to name for such internationally known and loved name brands as:

Capitol One

Kraft

Best Buy

Kodak

Puma

Honda

Kia

Saturn

Hershey's

Canon

Stouffer's

Boar's Head

How to Create a Name Millions Will Love

First, fill in the blank. I am the Greatest_____. If we skip this step we skip over our purpose and our unique gift to the world. It's so easy to get overwhelmed by the sheer volume of name possibilities. I often get asked, "*How do you know which name will ring true with your audience? Should the name explain all I do, or be about one specific aspect of my business? Should it be a broad metaphor, a coined name, lyrical, a call-to-action?*" Recently, a client asked, "*I'm doing so many different things under this one brand—how can I come up with a name that says it all?*"

The Ten Evidences Of Greatness

We're going digging for gold! Excavating evidence eliminates all of the confusion and the insecurities that naturally come up. Excavating evidence takes the pressure off you and puts your audience in the writer's chair. You see, ultimately your name needs to be the greatest story ever told. Now, who decides if it's the greatest story ever told? Not the teller. The audience does. So we're going to write your name as the greatest story in reverse by excavating evidence from your "audience."

To do this, you need to write down just five pieces of evidence you've collected that prove you're "The Greatest." I'm going to make it super easy for you and give you the ten types of evidence I use when I'm naming:

1. *Customer Loyalty*—Why do people come back to you?

2. *Positive Feedback*—You can dig up gold in your social media or in conversations you have with clients and customers.

3. *Common Requests*—What do people ask you to help them with?

4. *The Sum Up of You*—How do people introduce you to other colleagues? How do they sum up what you do?

5. *Effortless Mastery*—Are you able to do things that seem obvious to you but others get lost?

6. *Word-of-Mouth*—Have people shared your ideas with their friends? Which one gets shared the most?

7. *Movie Trailer*—Have you been telling people what you do and a friend interjects to add their favorite part of the story? That's the part that's resonating with people.

8. *Homage*—Have people adopted your ideas as their own? Which ones?

9. *Mimicry*—Have people adapted your services and applied them to their own business model?

10. Life Changers—Where have you had a positive impact?

- Emotional

- Financial

- Spiritual

- Physical

- Mental

Now that you've got your gold, I'm going to share with you exactly what I do when I name for companies like Hershey or Puma. You're going to need one of the greatest tools ever invented—your highlighter. I want you to go back over your evidence and highlight concepts that could be related to your name. Look for what makes you special, look for themes, metaphors, adjectives, and colors. Is your evidence full of action verbs or musicality? Become a detective for the common threads. Pick three prominent themes. This is now your *Name Map.* There's no need to get overwhelmed by naming when you've already got a ton of feedback from your community of potential customers on what resonates with them and you funnel it into three naming directions.

Let's say your three themes are: honesty, a feeling of victory, and dedication. You're going to brainstorm and spill out as many names as possible—at least thirty per creative direction—thirty names that are inspired by the concept of honesty, etc. . . By the end of this exercise you will have a solid list of 90 name candidates. Mix and match concepts to create unique names.

The Four Attractions of a Great Name

How do you decide what to name your company or product? Is it a gut decision? Do you ask a bunch of friends to see which one they like? What if you knew someone in the naming business and they had a proven way to select a winning name? You'd want it right? Good because I'm going to give it to you, right now. If I only had thirty minutes with my best friend to help them name their product, something they invest countless hours, thousands, even hundreds of thousands of dollars, and all of the priceless heart and soul into, I would share with them

The Four Attractions of a Great Name:

1. Emotion

2. Wish Fulfilled

3. Memorable

4. New but Familiar

#1—*Emotion*

Humans only make emotional decisions. There are no logical decisions. You can not ask anyone to invest in your product because if they want A, and B = A, therefore they must buy B. Neuroscientist Antonio Damasio made the discovery that people with the emotional centers of their brain damaged could not make decisions—even the simplest of decisions like what to eat. Humans are biologically unable to make decisions without emotions. Logic is largely used to make up a backstory as to why we decided to buy anything. But logic wasn't used to buy at all. The right name opens the right doors. If your name is a great description of what you do but is devoid of emotion, it's useless and it opens no doors—no emotion no buy.

#2—A Wish Fulfilled

What is the secret desire of your customers? What do they want but almost never say out loud. If you can speak in their language and give a voice to their secret wish, then they will feel seen by you, validated by you, loyal to you. It is a universal truth that if you can call out a future that others seek by name, they will follow you to it. Consider the "I Have a Dream" speech. *We* named it that. Dr. King didn't even have the "I have a dream" part in his speech. It's was improvised. But that was the phrase that moved us and that is what we collectively named his speech. You want a brand name that moves people to act because you have given a voice to what they have been thinking for some time, maybe their whole life. We are still following Martin Luther King into that future. Your name is the voice of your customer's wish being fulfilled. Paint a picture of their new future—do not describe the nuts and bolts.

#3—Memorable

There are some basics to making a name memorable. You want it to be easy to say, pronounce, spell, and share in most languages. Be sure to check an international dictionary to ensure your name doesn't offend an entire country! Ikea has a workbench named Fartful. Waterpik means morning erection in Danish. I'd go on but I'm too embarrassed!

But what is most memorable? When we hear a story we relax, we trust. A story is inherently disruptive, relevant, and visual. When we listen to a story is disrupts our pattern of thinking. We stop what we are thinking and listen to the story for relevance. How is this story relevant to me? We visualize every detail. Did you see the white coats? The half-paralyzed smile? When your name starts a story, your audience is more relaxed and eager to find out how this story will show them who they really are. Am I a Mac or a PC person? We learned to relax during a story from a very early age. *"Lie down, relax, and I'll tell you a bedtime story."*

Word-of-mouth advertising is the most effective form of advertising. How can you create a name that will inspire free word-of-mouth advertising? Let's dissect share-ability. What are you most likely to share from this chapter? Will you tell the story or will you recite the bullet points. Do you think when you put this book down you're more likely to remember the ten evidences of greatness, or that a name can save your life and bring you from "crippled for life" to a Miracle Man or Miracle Woman? I know you're a smart and savvy reader and you will be able to recite both. Well, let's say you share both the story and the bullet points with your friend. Which do you think your friend will share with their friend, the bullet points or the story? If you said the story you're right. Your Name must be *The Greatest Story Ever Told.*

#4—*The New Familiar*

Humans trust what is familiar. Trusting the familiar is what has enabled our species to survive. Our curiosity for the new is what has empowered us to thrive. You want an equal balance. When I spent five days in the Amazon, with no electricity, our canoe was our only form of transportation. There was in fact no road. There was only the Amazon.

If I was dropped off in the Amazon with no cabin, no picnic table, and no community, I would feel the tremendous threat of the new. I would retreat. But there was just enough familiar for me to venture forward to happily seek the new. I sought the sloths and monkeys, and with a machete in hand, I sought the remote trees whose pink sap eased sunburns. I began to feel elated and addicted to this new but familiar experience. I began to think, *"How much would it cost to build a home here?"* Have you ever priced homes in a new place where you were vacationing? This is the exact feeling you want to instill in your customers with your name. Enough "new" to excite and enough "familiar" for the prefrontal cortex to think. *"I could set up home here and thrive."* You want your customers to see your brand as their home.

Selecting A Great Name

Can you now see the secret power of naming? Consider that there has never been a community discovered though all of our travels around our planet that didn't instinctively name everything in their environment. Naming is the key to our survival and our evolution. When you choose the right name they will buy it in order to survive and thrive. You can inspire them to buy by emotionally conveying that your product will fulfill their wish. You can get free advertising with a name that is memorable and sharable. You can entice them to purchase your entire product suite with names that are a balance of new but familiar experiences.

Yes, the world is full of white coats naming you things you aren't, naming you into a small future. This is the day you say "No". I name my destiny. I will name my business into a greater future. I will name my products to create a greater future for all. My dream will not go through this life invisible.

Confucius says *"The man who says he can, and the man who says he can not . . . are both correct."* So which are you going to say about yourself?

You see, I'm looking for the creators, the inventors, the innovators, the entrepreneurs, because you are the ones who will make our world a better place for all. I'm only looking for those who have had enough of the white coats and who want to name their dream into a greater future. When you work with me, you join my family, and my family is made up of miracle men and miracle women. I know that inside you is the Miracle Man or Miracle Woman. I know you can express that at any time in your life as soon as you choose to do it. I can't make that choice for you. I can only tell you that the very best time to choose to name and grow rich is right now!

Canon's Special Offer:

• Get FREE word-of-mouth-advertising

• Get a .com name that *compels* your customers to *buy*

• Get the proven method to choose a final name that attracts millions

• Get the Free Video Series Today!

http://www.NameAndGrowRich.com

About Canon Wing

Canon Wing could be called the "6 Billion Dollar Namer." For 21 years she has named products for Fortune 500 companies like Nestle, Wendy's, Kraft, Samsung, Canon, Saturn, Kia, Discover Card, Kodak, Puma, Bayer and Honda. Her product names have been an influential driver of modern culture for over two decades. You have probably touched something Canon has named today. It's now her mission to illuminate, inspire, and instruct entrepreneurs to name their creations such that they call into being a greater future for all. The power of naming has been kept secret for too long. We all know that the right name opens the right doors but we must learn how to create the right name in order to Name And Grow Rich.

To find out more about Canon, visit:
http://www.NameAndGrowRich.com

Chapter 6

7 Steps to Emails that Make Friends and Influence People
by Michele Camacho

Do you remember the moments in your life when you had a spontaneous thought, the kind that seemed so far-fetched you wondered where it came from . . . and then later it came true? Well, that's how it was for me and email marketing. *"If only I could make money writing emails in my pajamas!"* popped into my head, and the baby kicked, as if in agreement. I closed my laptop, and drifted to sleep counting emails bursting with money.

By morning, my perception of possibilities had broken open. In a moment of clarity, I decided to forgo my search for another engineering job, and embark on the entrepreneurial journey.

Within days I had two clients, and was working from home on my own schedule. That was the beginning of crafting email and website copy. I was astonished to find that others struggled to write what comes naturally to me.

By grace, I was soon trained personally by Tracy Repchuk. When she told me the email campaign I wrote was the best submittal she'd ever received, I knew I found a way to help you get the most from every email—with messages that engage, enlighten, and convert—so that everything you say is like a money magnet.

Effective emails have to be crafted specifically to make money—you deserve it! Follow the steps I lay out here, and you will have a solid foundation on which to build profits. The basics aren't complicated; once you know what they are, they will seem totally intuitive. Even if you've written newsletters for years, don't skip this. You'd be amazed what a difference some tweaking makes. *Here's to Your Prosperity!*

Step 1—How Emails Make You Money

Simply put, you make money when someone clicks on a link and makes a purchase. This is called "conversion." To boost profits, make clicking fast, easy, and urgent.

Start with the End in Mind

Before you start typing away, be crystal clear on what action you want someone to take. Make sure this "call-to-action" either solves a problem or feeds a passion, and is specifically relevant to your target market. By doing this first, your email marketing is more likely to become a money magnet.

Why Clicks

Your call-to-action will typically be to click a link, because it is something someone can do immediately, and you can test the effectiveness of your email by monitoring the "click-through rate."

Need Some Call to Action Ideas?

Invite them to:

- Download your free guide
- Go to the sales page of your high priced product
- Register for your free webinar;
- Fill out a survey
- "Like" your Facebook fanpage
- Buy one of your affiliate products
- Download free software
- Buy tickets to your live event
- Read your blog post
- Subscribe to your YouTube channel
- Purchase access to your membership site

Clicks Convert Passive Readers to Active Buyers

Did you also notice that some of the calls-to-action ideas listed above are for free stuff? Giving links to fun, free, and money saving stuff trains people to click with pleasure. Later, when your link is to a high-priced product, they are more likely to click to the sales page out of habit. With every click they are unconsciously saying *"Yes, I like this," "Yes, I trust you," "Yes, this is worth my time," "Yes, I want more,"* and ultimately, *"Yes, here is my credit card!"*

***Awesome*!** You know how to make money with a call-to-action! Now turn your attention to your target market—let's go!

Step 2—Answer *"What's In it for Me?"*

Unless you are a celebrity, people aren't all that interested in you—they're asking *"What's in it for me?"* Everything you write has to answer that question. To make it about them, get to know them.

Define Your Target Market

Even awesome emails will go unread if they are written for the wrong audience. An aggressive style may work for a male audience, whereas a nurturing tone fits your female audience.

Who's your target market? Is it women entrepreneurs, age 45-60, in the holistic field? Is it male CEO's, age 45-60, with over 500 employees, who value team building?

Know Their Wants and Needs

The more narrowly you define your target market, the easier it will be to research the problems they have, the words they use, and the passions that enliven them. Your ability to solve issues that rob their sleep with worry makes your emails more personal, and your services more valuable.

7 Steps to Emails that Make Friends and Influence People

Write for Humans Who Act on Emotion

Your emails are not the place to write for search engines. Always remember that a feeling, breathing, human with a full range of emotion is deciding whether or not to open your email and click.

Your Story, Their Life

Engaging with story is a powerful way to make your experience about their lives. Help them identify with your triumphs, and connect the dots . . . if you did it, so can they. This is a personal way to grant them the strength and courage to take a leap and make a change; and who better to help them than you?

Amazing! You feel you are already friends with your target market! Up next: how to cultivate trust with people you've never met!

Step 3—Build Trusting Relationships

Even though email marketing is the electronic equivalent of sending bulk mail, there are ways to make it personal. Building trust from the very start is essential; otherwise people won't sign up, will unsubscribe, or will mark your email as spam.

Get Permission to Put Someone's Email on Your List

Maintain high integrity by never buying or selling a list of email addresses. Such practices will harm your business; people feel violated by emails they never requested.

Have them enter their name and email in an opt-in form that clearly states what they are signing up for.

Get on a First Name Basis

Collect someone's first name at the same time as getting their email address—you'll need it to personalize your emails.

Your name is also important! Don't hide behind a product name—be seen and be proud! Leverage your signature to make a personal connection.

Give a Gift

What better way to answer *"What's in it for me?"* than with a gift? Write a guide book of tips, to give as a free gift for the privilege of getting someone's name and email. Make sure your gift is of real value, immediately benefits them, and showcases you as an expert.

Don't skimp on the quality; it's their first impression of your work!

Whew! You wrote your free guide and your opt-in is all set up! Hmmm . . . How do you tackle writing volumes of emails?

Step 4—Convert with Campaigns

Take a "campaign" approach, and write emails in series with focused intentions. This will give you structure, and tie your emails into your overall marketing strategy.

7 Steps to Emails that Make Friends and Influence People

Coming Up with Content

Instead of wracking your brains for new material, start with repurposing things you've already written, such as your free guide. Build from what you've got to focus on clear business objectives, such as: website registration, product launch, book launch, holiday promotion, affiliate sales, video series, etc. Here's a closer look:

Your First Email Campaign—The Gift that Keeps on Giving!

When people opt-in, the objective of your first campaign is to build a trusting relationship by leveraging the free guide you gave when they signed up.

Each email highlights the benefit of one of the tips, with a link to the guide to see the full instruction. Each message is like a high-powered, bite-sized mini coaching session. While adding value, they learn what you do, why they need it, and how to take the next step.

Your Live Event Campaign

Whether your live event is a webinar or face-to-face workshop, a full email campaign is critical to your efforts. At a minimum, you will need emails to invite people to the event, confirm registration, remind them not to miss it, and thank them for attending.

Are you upselling to a high-priced product with a special limited-time offer? Weave that in as well. Oh, and prepare emails for friends to promote to their lists!

Excellent! You have a campaign plan with clear business goal! All you have to do now is craft emails that get opened and clicked!

Step 5—Email-Opening Subject Lines and Deal-Closing PS's

Each element of your email message serves a specific function. Leveraging how the subject line and the PS play off of one another can improve your email's open and click-through rates.

Email Bookends

The subject line gets your email opened, and the PS gets the call-to-action clicked. Although you will spend considerably more time crafting the subject line, first write a clear-call-to action for the PS. This makes it easier for the subject line to match the message.

Tell Them Everything They Need to Know

Some people have just a few seconds to scan an email before moving on. Make it fast and easy for them to open and click, just based on the subject line and PS.

The subject line should be brief, yet convey the essence of your message. The PS briefly says what to do, with a link. Both should answer *"What's in it for me?"* and why it's urgent.

7 Steps to Emails that Make Friends and Influence People

Why Subject Lines are More Important than Content

If someone never opens your email, they will never click the call-to-action inside. For this reason, many experienced copywriters say you should even spend twice as much time reviewing your email's subject line than its content!

Create Urgency for Instant Opens and Clicks

One way to create urgency is through scarcity. When you offer overwhelming value for a limited time, availably, pricing, or access, it creates a sense that if they don't act now, they will miss out.

Another way to create urgency is by triggering an emotional response, such as pain, pleasure, hope, passion, humor, or curiosity. Research your niche to know their triggers.

Fantastic! Your subject line and PS rock. It's time to craft content!

Step 6—Write for Speed-Readers on Mobile Devices

Formatting your emails for fast reading and easy clicking on small screens is crucial to making more money.

Mobile Mania

What are people doing when they get your email? Very likely they are on a mobile device, in the midst of doing something else, such as shopping, eating, waiting in line, or having a conversation. You have only seconds to make an impact.

Easy to Read

To make your messages easy on the eyes,
don't go all the way across page.
Shorter lines are faster to read and navigate,
especially on a mobile phone.
Like this paragraph—see how it works?

Easy to Click

Make the link really obvious and easy to click, on a line by itself. You can even give readers the link a couple times—towards the top and then towards the bottom of your message.

Just One Call-to-Action

Focus on just one call-to-action per email. If you ask them to do two different things, neither will get done. If you feel strongly about the second call-to-action, it deserves its own email.

Have a Lot to Say?

Remember, scarcity creates urgency. Instead of a long newsletter that they will leave for later and forget, move your content to your blog. In the email give just a teaser, with a link to the specific blog post to "read more".

Incredible! Your campaign is designed for fast-track marketing! But will it pass the test of time?

Step 7—Make It Always Feel Like the First Time

Your email messages should always sound fresh and current, even when written years ago.

Suspension of Disbelief

Even though people know they're getting automated messages, many will suspend disbelief and read them as if you had personally written to them, which is what you're striving for! Don't offend your audience with an email that is blatantly outdated; the validity of your advice may be doubted, and trust in you weakened.

The Evergreen Concept

An evergreen tree looks green and plush year round, when other trees are looking bare and scraggly. This perennial staying power is an excellent model for the emails that stay in your queue.

The Freshness Test

After you craft an email, pretend three years have gone by and read it through again—still sound fresh? Be wary of time references, such as *"I just gave my first TV appearance..."* If now there are twenty TV appearances on your media page, something will feel "off" to them.

You Change Over Time, and So Should Your Emails

No matter how good you get at evergreen writing, periodically review your messages. Keep them consistent with your online presence as your branding and products evolve.

Give Special Attention to Your Welcome Series

New subscribers get the oldest messages first, so make sure the initial campaign, in particular, is always current. This is when you are first building a relationship, and trust in you is most fragile.

    Fantastic! You're all set, or are you? Copywriting is a real craft, and there is so much more I want to teach you! How does a *free*, **No-Risk Email Marketing Review** sound?

MICHELE CAMACHO

Email Marketing that Creates Massive Results

Email and Campaign Copywriting Creating Massive Marketing Results

Michele's Special Offer:

For a limited time, let Michele help you with a
Free Email Marketing Review

Michele will re-write one email for *free*,
with permission that your email be
used as a before/after example.

To access this offer, contact Michele directly at:

Michele@MicheleCamacho.com

About Michele Camacho

Michele Camacho is an award-winning Email and Campaign Copywriter, who helps results-oriented entrepreneurs get the most from every email, with messages that engage, enlighten, and convert, so that everything you say is like a money magnet.

A natural story teller, Michele is published by *Chicken Soup for the Soul*, chosen from thousands of submissions. She leverages her story skills to write marketing emails for clients—because prospects will remember your story more than your product.

Michele was personally trained in email marketing by Tracy Repchuk; international best-selling author and world's top woman speaker for online structure and social media marketing. Michele uses the same copywriting approach that Tracy uses in her own multimillion-dollar Internet empire; engage and convert through story.

Michele focuses on the higher purpose of a good email marketing campaign, which is to enlighten, serve, and provide your prospects with the greatest experience when you connect with them.

She has a knack for making it all about your prospects by minimizing the self-referencing "*I*." They enjoy the emails more and you make more money.

Connect with Michele on social media through theses links:

Facebook: http://www.Facebook.com/MicheleCamachoS

LinkedIn: http://www.LinkedIn.com/in/MicheleCamacho

Twitter: http://www.Twitter.com/MicheleCamachoS

YouTube: http://www.YouTube.com/user/MicheleCamachoS

Google +: http://www.gplus.to/MicheleCamacho

Email: Michele@MicheleCamacho.com

**To find out more about Michele, visit:
http://www.MicheleCamacho.com and
http://www.MakeMoneyWithEmailMarketing.com**

Chapter 7

The Health of Your Business
by Susie Garcia, RDN

We have all heard the saying, *"She's the picture of health,"* but have you really thought about what that picture looks like? Think about it for a moment. When you "picture" a healthy person, what does that person look like? Do you see yourself?

The health of your business truly revolves around the health of *you*. How healthy do you appear? If you didn't see yourself when you pictured a healthy person, why not? It may be because you have some health goals you still want to achieve, so don't be too hard on yourself. However, it's important to consider your own personal health as a vital part of your business. If you don't picture yourself as healthy, chances are others don't either, and that perception can translate to a perception about your business being in not-so-great health.

Consider the first impression you make. It could be at a networking event, a client meeting, a training workshop, or a coffee meeting with a colleague.

How do you show up? Are you tired and worn out, or running late and frantic? Are you complaining about lack of sleep? Are you telling people you were so busy you didn't even eat lunch? How you show up mentally and physically are just as important (and sometimes more!) than whether or not you are wearing a designer suit and expensive shoes. If you see yourself in the previous examples, chances are you are not taking care of your personal health, which is going to make it difficult to run an effective business. Not only because others' perceptions may deter them from doing business with you, but also it's harder to work efficiently when your energy level is low.

Please note that when I'm referring to a "healthy person," I don't mean you need to look like a professional athlete! It means your eyes are bright, your skin is healthy, you have a bounce in your step, and your energy level is high and contagious. However, for your own benefit you should strive to keep your weight within the recommended range.

I was recently reading a top forty business women's list in a leading business magazine, and based on their headshots, I would estimate that over 80 percent of the women appeared to be at a healthy weight. It's possible that when people see top level executives or entrepreneurs appearing to be at healthy weights, they may then expect a successful person to appear in a similar fashion. I believe the appearance of health is even more critical if you are in a health and wellness industry; your appearance is part of your credibility. If you are in the process of a transformation because of a lifestyle change (for example, you started using a product you are selling and are losing weight), be sure to share that right away when you meet someone!

When I work with clients, I emphasize the importance of nourishing their bodies properly, and there are certain things you should do daily to nourish your business properly. I've outlined four key areas—*scheduling, activity, focus, and R&R*.

Nourishing Your Body—*Scheduling*

Eat breakfast! Have something to eat within two hours of waking. This will start your metabolism and fuel your *mind* and body to start the day! We've all seen the advertisements that tout the benefits of breakfast and academic performance for children. Guess what? It's the same for grown-ups! Our brains need food to function.

Many of my former breakfast-skipping clients would tell me that when they don't eat, they don't get hungry. If you too are traditionally a breakfast skipper, you probably have noticed that when you actually eat something—like a piece of toast—a few hours later your stomach starts to growl. Guess what? That means your metabolism is working! If you push through until lunch without eating, you are training your metabolism to run slower. Our metabolisms are already slowing down as we get older, so do what you can to offset it!

You may find that you have time to grab something quickly in the morning, and if it's not a lot of food, allow yourself a snack mid-morning to complete the meal. Be sure to include protein at breakfast, it will make the meal last longer.

Eat something every four to five hours and don't skip meals. Eating during the day is when you need the calories the most, not at the end of the day when you are winding down and are less active. You may actually have to set a timer to make sure you eat. I certainly have had times when I'm working on a project, and suddenly realize it's lunch time! I am less than twenty steps away from my kitchen when I'm in my home office, and I'm sure many entrepreneurs experience the same thing. You just have to make yourself step away from your desk and nourish your body.

If you can, try to eat every four to five hours and limit snacks. I don't recommend grazing all day unless you have a very active profession like that of a personal trainer, aerobics instructor, or some other physically demanding job. Be cognizant not to go more than six hours between meals. When this happens, you diminish your ability to make a good choice, because, darn it, you're hungry! Then everything looks good! Poor meal timing is often the culprit of business professionals gaining weight over a few years, and it also can be the success of losing that weight gradually and keeping it off!

Nourishing Your Business—*Scheduling*

Schedule your day. Make sure you know what you are planning to do each day and be realistic about your "To-Do-List". There are many systems available for time management; pick what works for you, not necessarily what works for someone else. One thing I have found to be very helpful is to pay attention to how long it takes me to complete a task. That way, when I'm writing my to-do-list, I can include an estimate of how long it is going to take me to complete each task. For example, I know that if I want to publicize an event, like a webinar, that it will take me an hour. That may seem like a long time, but I actually kept track of how long it took me and there were a lot of steps!

- Add the event to my own calendar.

- Create a webinar Registration page, which includes writing a description of the event.

- Create the event on Facebook, add an event photo, and share and invite friends.

The Health of Your Business

- Write blog post about the event including a link to the registration page.

- Ping the blog with ping-ing software.

- Send an email blast promoting the event.

There are two things you can do to help estimate your time and improve the efficiency of your day. The next time you do a task that you repeat often (checking email, writing an article, calling ten clients etc. . . .), time yourself! Record your results somewhere so you can add future tasks to the list. Even if you don't have records for all tasks, the next time you write your to-do-list, start estimating times (I like to over-estimate), and then decide on which day you are going to do each task based on other meetings and appointments.

Schedule money-making opportunities at least three days per week. Analyze your week; if everything you are doing is marketing and administrative and you don't block out time to meet with paying clients or make sales calls to get more paying clients, your business won't survive.

A money-making activity means that you are either getting paid for that time or you are prospecting/selling to get paid in the future. Listening to a recording on increasing your sales is *not* a money-making activity, it's training. Attending a Chamber of Commerce mixer is *not* a money-making activity, it's networking. You may be thinking that only three days a week of money-making opportunities isn't enough, however, the goal is to have more than one appointment/opportunity on each of those three days! I perform much better in all areas—money-making, administrative, networking, and training—if I chunk them together instead of trying to do all of them every day.

I've found Wednesdays and Thursdays are the best days for me to meet with clients, whether in person or virtually, so I will schedule several clients on each of those days. Many years ago when I first started my practice, I tried to be over-accommodating and would fit clients in any day they requested, but found I was not being very efficient. When I state I make appointments on Wednesdays and Thursdays, it still works out. I use Friday as my third day and call it *Follow-up Friday*; this is when I make calls or send emails to follow up with prospects and clients to create more sales.

Nourishing Your Body—*Activity*

Regular physical exercise and activity are vital to being and feeling healthy and vibrant.

Stand up more. There are dramatic studies that show how detrimental sitting can be to your health; it actually increases the fat deposited around your heart. You burn more calories when you stand and it helps improve your posture. My favorite tips to stand more include:

- Utilize a standing work station; even if it is your kitchen counter.

- Stand up to take phone calls, and walk around a little bit if you can (another benefit to this tip is that you won't be checking emails while you are on the phone and your caller has your full attention).

- Take a short "walk around" break for five minutes every hour.

- Use an exercise ball to sit on to activate more muscle groups.

Even if you are not trying to lose weight, standing is a great way to be healthier!

Schedule your work-outs. Make an appointment with yourself and put it on your calendar to walk, run, go to the gym, or go to an exercise class. Because I am in the health industry, I believe it is part of my job to exercise. If I'm suggesting that my clients do something, I should be walking the walk (literally!). I pick out a couple of yoga classes each week and put them on my calendar. I schedule classes with my trainer, and even block out times that I'm going to run.

There is a caption on a cartoon I use in presentations that reads, *"What fits into your busy schedule better, exercising one hour a day or being dead twenty-four hours a day?"* It makes you pause and think, doesn't it? Even if you start out scheduling a fifteen-minute walk, three times next week, if it's on your calendar you'll be more likely to stick to it. Scheduling exercise with another person is great for motivation and accountability. I try to schedule a walk with people I meet networking, instead of a coffee meeting.

Nourishing Your Business—*Activity*

Stand out more. Know and be confident in your brand, whether it's "brand you" or a company you represent. At the end of the day people will buy *you*. One of the most effective ways to broadcast your brand is to stand out on the Internet. Do you have your *Unique Selling Proposition* (USP), a landing page, and a great website? Tracy Repchuk repeatedly says that once someone meets you in person, the next thing they will do is check you out online. You need to make sure you are standing out online as well as in person! Jim Meskiman and Nadine LaJoie's chapters will give you amazing ideas for standing out in person!

Schedule your networking. Are you actively marketing your business and are you out in front of people so they know who you are? If you are in the growing stage of your business, you have to get out and network (see Sam Rafoss' chapter for great tips). However, you need to be strategic when selecting networking groups, and you may have to visit a few to find the right one. Just like scheduling your workouts, schedule your networking and determine how many hours each week you can invest. It's easy to get caught up in attending networking meetings and scheduling "coffee meetings." These are important activities for most entrepreneurs, but you have to leave time in your schedule to actually see a paying client!

Nourishing Your Body—*Focus*

It may seem daunting to incorporate every healthy habit into your life right now, so I'd like to suggest two areas of focus that can help you become the picture of health.

Eat More Vegetables

Vegatables provide your richest source for nutrients. I can't emphasize enough the importance of a diet rich in lots of veggies! Please notice I didn't say *fruits and vegetables*. Fruits are great to include, but too much fruit equals too much sugar. Current research is revealing the detrimental inflammatory effects of sugar and how it contributes to *so* many diseases, including heart disease, so a couple of servings of fruit a day is plenty. Vegetables* on the other hand, are limitless. Go for ten servings if you can! Keep in mind one serving is only one-half cup cooked or one cup raw, so it isn't as hard as you might think! Vegetables are rich in phytonutrients and anti-oxidants that you just can't get from a vitamin capsule; which means they help protect you against cancer, heart disease, and digestive problems—the benefits are too many to list! Here are some ideas of where you can add more vegetables:

BREAKFAST

- Omelet
- Protein drink/smoothie

LUNCH

- Add to a wrap or sandwich (lettuce, tomato, cucumber, red pepper)
- Soup (make a big batch—I love adding cabbage and spinach)

DINNER

- Salad or crudités before dinner
- Grind up spinach or zucchini in sauces
- Cauliflower with mashed potatoes
- Sauté onions, garlic, and peppers. Serve with meats

Does not include starchy vegetables—corn, peas, potatoes, or sweet potatoes.

Stay Hydrated

Did you know that if you are dehydrated by as little as two percent, it can decrease your short-term memory by seven to twelve percent?

Water is the purest form of hydration, but all fluids are important to your hydration status. Ideally, you should choose fluids that are calorie free (without artificial sweeteners) and caffeine free. So, for example, coffee is a fluid, however it contains caffeine and is acidic so often the net result is a dehydrating effect. Herbal teas, on the other hand, do not have the same effect, even if they have a little caffeine. Sparkling water with or without a citrus or fruit essence can be a great way to increase fluids; try putting sparkling water in a wine glass for dinner—it will make it more special!

How much should you drink? It depends on how much you weigh; the closer you can get to drinking half of your weight (in pounds) in ounces of fluid the better! For example, if you weigh 150 pounds, that would be 75 ounces of fluid. I encourage you to hydrate more each day and notice how your energy level improves! Your joints may be less achy which will make adding activity easier!

Nourishing Your Business—*Focus*

It can seem equally as daunting to do everything you think you "should" for marketing your business online. Where do you start, Facebook, more tweets? Do you need Pinterest, or YouTube videos?

Keep more clients happy—your richest source for referrals. When you start trying to focus on marketing to many different target audiences, you will simply confuse everyone, including yourself. If you already have clients and want more, be sure to keep your current clients happy, because they will *refer* more business to you, which means you don't have to do crazy, all over the place marketing.

If you don't nurture your current clients, they will lose interest in working with you and you won't even enter their mind when they encounter someone who needs your help. Or, worse yet, they recommend *not* using you.

Think about something you could easily do for current or past clients to keep connected. Maybe it's sending a birthday card, or having a special email blast specific to clients, instead of to everyone on your list. (See Michele Camacho's chapter for great ideas on copywriting to reach your audience.)

Stay social—don't neglect social media. Stay on top of two or three social media platforms. Depending on your industry the platforms may differ, but if you are trying to do a lot of things yourself, then to do everything all at once on social media is a huge undertaking. Commit to three (or maybe only two for now) things, and if you can, set them up to blast to several sites simultaneously. For example, I set up my blog posts to automatically share on Twitter, LinkedIn, Google +, and Facebook, so by focusing on regular blogging I'm getting exposure on three additional platforms. You may want to go back and re-read Tracy's chapter about social media to hone in on where to focus.

Nourishing Your Body—*R & R (Rest & Relaxation)*

Get enough sleep. My clients sometimes wonder why their nutritionist is asking them if they get enough sleep. I do have a holistic approach, but there is also science behind the question.

Think about a time when you were returning from a trip or were up all night with a sick child, and the next day you were exhausted and hungry, almost like you just couldn't get enough to eat and were eating all day. A couple of things happen. Because food is energy, your body is looking for some type of energy when really you just need sleep. But there are also two hormones that change when we get a good night's sleep or not enough sleep.

When you get a good night's sleep (usually at least seven hours), a hormone called Leptin is increased. Leptin actually suppresses food intake. In other words, you will feel more satisfied with less food and won't want to snack all day. Alternatively, the hormone Ghrelin increases with sleep deprivation (even just one night) and Ghrelin plays a role in meal initiation, or the hunger response. So the less sleep you get, the more Ghrelin you produce, and the more often during the day you are going to feel hungry. Can you go to bed thirty minutes earlier? I bet you can! Try it tonight!

Pause—take a breath. Right now, as soon as you read the next sentence with the directions, just do it. Set down the book (or the electronic device you are reading it on). If you can, put your arms out to the side; take a deep breath in through your nose and bring your arms up above your head, then exhale through your mouth and bring your arms back down. Do it three times.

Ahhh, wasn't that nice? Even without the arm movement, pausing to breath increases oxygen to your brain, but it also gives your mind a chance to slow down. Give yourself permission to take a three-breath break every hour!

I was working with a high-level executive with a tech company who sat at a desk all day. He told me he would be so hungry in the afternoon that he couldn't resist eating something (and of course there was a mountain of free food available in the cafeteria and snack room). Because his job was very busy and high pressure, his mind was constantly spinning and it created a craving for food, which was in essence, a break. He incorporated breathing more often and noticed he didn't have the same sensation of hunger! I see the same thing with entrepreneurs trying to do so many things. If you can let your mind rest, you can refocus and also reduce food cravings.

Nourishing Your Business—*R & R (Rest & Relaxation)*

Get enough personal time. It's often hard to let yourself relax and not just work, work, work. And there are times in your business when you may have to keep a crazy schedule for a few weeks to push ahead, but if you don't create some balance and take care of yourself, you aren't being healthy. I mentioned at the beginning of the chapter that the health of your business depends on the health of *you*. If you work from a home office, defining the end of your day, and not continuing to check emails, post on Facebook, and write your to-do-list into the late evening can be a challenge.

If you aren't sure if this is a problem for you, pay attention to what your spouse/significant other, or children are saying. If you hear a lot of complaints about the time you spend working, chances are you are neglecting your personal time, which includes time with family and friends.

Perhaps you're super driven and you just can't help it—then schedule your personal time just like you schedule your meetings and workouts! Schedule lunch with a friend, a massage, a date night. You will actually notice that when you stop working, and stop the spinning and thinking about everything, when you come back to a project it will flow!

Pause . . . set your intention and have a goal for your marketing, networking, and business activity. This pause in your business could be a couple of minutes in the car before you go into a meeting with a potential new client, to think about what result you want of the meeting instead of just showing up without much of a plan. This pause in your business might be setting aside several hours or even a day to work on your Unique Selling Proposition (USP) or another part of your business that just isn't done, and that causes you frustration. This pause could be a monthly phone call with your accountant or bookkeeper to review your budget. This pause could be a few seconds of thought before you answer someone's question to make sure you answer it correctly. This pause could be a daily meditation or affirmation to create positive energy. ***The devil might be in the details, but sometimes your progress is in the pause.***

I know you will move forward in health, for you and your business!

Susie Garcia
Practical Healthy Solutions That Fit Your Lifestyle

Susie's Special Offer:

Receive Susie's step-by-step guide,
7 Simple Steps to a Healthier You
with practical tips you can implement right away
to improve your health and well being at:
http://www.YourHealthyLifeChoices.com

About Susie Garcia, RDN

Susie Garcia is an Award-winning Registered Dietitian and Nutritionist, Healthy Lifestyle Coach, Author, National Speaker, Food Industry Consultant, Menu and Meal Planning Expert, Sports Nutrition Consultant and Corporate Wellness Advisor.

She is supporting others and making an impact to address better food habits, healthier living, and creating a culture of empowered eaters.

Susie received the prestigious Recognized Young Dietitian of the Year Award from the Academy of Nutrition & Dietetics and the Texas Dietetic Association and recently was the recipient of the Amazing Impact Award from the Inspirational Business Leaders Council.

Susie is Founder and Owner of Nutrition for Your Lifestyle in the San Francisco Bay Area and works with individuals and companies throughout the country.

She is co-author of Psyched to be Skinny and has appeared on ABC, CBS, and FOX affiliate television stations, NPR affiliate Radio, internet radio and filmed over twenty healthy cooking videos for eHow.com

**To find out more about Susie, visit:
http://www.TheSusieGarcia.com and
http://www.YourHealthyLifeChoices.com**

Chapter 8

Connecting Your Business for Global Impact
by Alberto Liberal

Before we delve into the contents of this chapter, I thought I'd give you a quick glimpse into my background. After all, it helps to know the pen behind the words, right?

I have over nineteen years of experience in business, with a strong understanding of business, economics, auditing, and management control. My professional background allowed me to acquire and develop plenty of "in-the-trenches" experience in all areas of business, as a leader in the financial sector.

I started off in my work at a small consultant company, as an international business consultant, and gradually moved up to multinational companies, where I managed business units.

Throughout my life, I lead myself within these five values:

1. *Beauty*—surround myself with great people, great books, positive vibes, whatever it is I believe is beauty.

2. *Passion*—this is crucial to me. That's the foundation of my why . . . the why I do every single day.

3. *Authenticity*—is me, the real me, and how I present myself to the world around me. It starts with myself, being

true and authentic to me, which reflects my outcome to others.

4. *Freedom*—meaning being a free spirit within the inner power to fly towards my dreams.

5. *Excellence*—last but not the least I strongly believe in excellence, the attitude of putting every part of myself into achieving what I purpose to do.

Long story short, I've enjoyed a lot of success in this field and am now ready to give it back to the community.

This chapter is primarily aimed at passionate entrepreneurs and business owners who recognize that the world we live in is full of opportunities, and who are prepared to do their very best to make use of these opportunities to propel their business to the top.

In the forthcoming pages, I am going to reveal how you can transform your business to have a global impact. This transformation is based on proven and tested principles and techniques you can apply for rapid results in your business, to transform your profits.

I am going to take you on a journey where you can benefit from my knowledge and experience, so *you* also can take your company to the next level and enjoy massive success in the exciting world of business. Let's get started!

Forward Thinking—New Economy, New Mindset

"The world is changing very fast. Big will not beat small anymore. It will be the fast beating the slow."
-Rupert Murdoch

Let's face it, the rules for business have changed, and those who are quick to adapt to the shift will be the ones who will ultimately prosper in this new, competitive, and more global financial environment.

The Internet in general, and social media in particular, both play a significant role in the current business landscape, so you need to keep on top of technology also.

Today, the focus is mostly on the customer and the kind of user experience you're able to offer him. You need to see things from his perspective, deliver to him amazing value and top class service, and make sure you've got superb systems in place to make his experience with your company a memorable one.

You must know what's going on in your niche, identify new and upcoming trends, network regularly, and always strive to differentiate yourself from your competitors.

Here are two key strategies on how you can achieve this:

1. Build Relationships

Aim to form stable, long-term relationships with your customers. Reward loyal clients by offering them exclusive deals and discounts. Let them know you value their business and you're glad to have them on board. Listen to their suggestions and feedback and then deliver exactly what they ask for. After all, the customer is king!

2. Innovate

It's not likely that many of us can be as innovative as Apple or Google, but we can all come up with new and innovative ideas to help us stand out from the crowd. Innovation need not be complex; in fact, it can be as simple as delivering pizza within thirty minutes guaranteed, or providing banking services 24/7/365. In other words, don't take your foot off the pedal, and never take your customers or employees—or even success—for granted. Always raise your game, set the bar higher, and blow your competition away!

Select Your Market, Shape Your Target

Given the present state of the economy, as well as the fiercely competitive nature of the business world, having a well-defined target audience has become more vital than ever.

Many companies state they sell to *"anyone that's interested in what we offer."* Some of them say they target pensioners, stay-at-home moms, college students, or pet owners. All of these markets are too general. However, targeting a specific audience doesn't mean you have to exclude customers who don't fit your criteria; rather, precision marketing enables you to invest your time and marketing dollars on a specific group more likely to purchase what you're selling. This is a much more practical and effective way to reach prospective customers and generate sales.

Now, you might be wondering... *"How do I dig up all this information?"* Browse through forums, blogs, and magazine articles that "talk" about your ideal customer. Hop on to social media platforms where people in your target group communicate with each other. Conduct a survey.

Either way, you can save money and get a better ROI by accurately defining your target market and knowing what makes them tick.

Define Your Message

As an entrepreneur or business owner, no one understands your brand better than you do. Furthermore, as you travel along the bumpy and exciting journey of entrepreneurship, you probably think that explaining why you love your products/services—and why your target audience should love them also—should be a breeze.

Unfortunately, though, it's not all that simple. You see, in order to get people excited about what you offer, you first have to make them understand it. The problem is you're fighting against an average attention span that only lasts for a few seconds.

So how do you get customers to sit up and pay attention to your message amidst a sea of distraction? By crafting a message that's brief, relevant, and most importantly, captivating.

Follow the steps outlined below to identify and define your key messages and narrow them into a compelling one-liner that'll grab (and maintain) the interest of your target market.

The 4 Ws

The four most important questions you must ask yourself when you craft your statement should begin with *"Who?"* *"What?"* *"Why?"* and *"Where?"* This is the valuable information you will need to convey to your audience within seconds, so they realize what you're offering is worth their time. To begin, jot down the answers to the questions below:

- What does your business do?

- What need/desire does it fulfill?

- What is your USP (Unique Selling Proposition)? In other words, what do you offer that your competition doesn't?

- Who is your audience? (It helps to draw up a detailed customer profile.)

Your Message

Once you have everything written down, challenge yourself to describe your business in just one sentence. Refer to your notes and cherry-pick the most crucial information and combine it with some of your favorite words and phrases. Oh, and avoid clichés! They are boring and overused. For a little inspiration, check out these examples of companies with fantastic mission statements:

Airbnb:

Airbnb is a trusted community marketplace for people to list, discover, and book unique accommodations around the world—online or from a mobile phone.

HowAboutWe:

HowAboutWe is the fastest, easiest, most fun way to go on awesome dates.

Artsicle:

Artsicle is here to help you discover your personal taste in art, from the comfort of your couch.

Keep it simple! Your statement needs to be written in the voice of your brand. Your statement must be clear, to the point, and compelling to anyone who sees/hears it.

Positioning

People queue up for many different things—to snag the latest iPhone model, to purchase tickets to the most talked-about movie in town, to get an autograph of their favorite author—and obviously, the best place to be in any queue is always right at the front.

You must think of your business the same way. Regardless of the product/service you're selling and promoting, when potential customers decide to make a purchase, your business needs to be at the top of their minds.

Here's how to make that happen on a global level:

> **Tip #1:** Reduce your dependence on local markets. Some of the ways you can safeguard your business from experiencing a decline in local sales is by exporting, selling online, and offering franchising opportunities.

> **Tip #2:** Venture into emerging markets. Countries such as Malaysia, India, and China offer immense growth potential for businesses big and small, and you can easily increase your revenue by tapping and penetrating into these profitable markets.

> **Tip #3:** Create a Strategic Global Alliance (SGA). In a nutshell, an SGA is a partnership that's established between two (or more) businesses to achieve a common goal, with the agreement to share expertise, resources,

and risk. This is an excellent strategy to enter a new market and begin profiting in a short period of time, while reducing the competition you may face from other already established companies.

Tip #4: Aggressively promote your business online. Make use of popular social media platforms (eg: Twitter, LinkedIn, and Facebook) to market your merchandise to a worldwide audience—in the languages they speak and understand.

When you put these techniques into action, you'll be right on track to positioning your business as the leader in your niche—not just locally, but also internationally.

Alliances Worldwide

Once you've built up a close network of business associates, it's time to leverage these contacts in a way that can help you take your business to the next level.

How do you go about doing this? Simple . . .you form solid *strategic global alliances* through the power of affiliates.

The *affiliate marketing* route is one of the smartest and easiest ways to increase publicity and skyrocket sales. With an affiliate program, you pay someone a commission (i.e. a percentage of the total sale) for them to sell your product/service. And when implemented online, it enables a small business to have an international workforce without having to spend top dollar to maintain a physical staff globally.

Determine Which of Your Products can be Sold by Others

Here's a good rule to keep in mind: if there's a huge demand for what you're marketing, and you've got an excellent offer that successfully meets and fulfils this demand, create an affiliate program for it. It's as simple as that!

Figure out the Percentage of profits You're Willing to Give to your Affiliates

Study the profit margins on every single product you're selling. Then, work out how much you will pay someone who sells it for you. Or, take a look at the commissions being offered by your competitors and match their rates—or go one better than them and devise a better pay structure so their affiliates start selling your products!

What Method of Payment Do You Plan to Use?

You could either provide affiliates with a flat fee or a percentage of each sale they make. Just make sure it's an attractive sum that will be worth their while.

Decide on Your Payment Threshold

Requiring your affiliates to generate a certain amount of sales before qualifying for payment is a surefire way to turn them off. Instead, pay them often (e.g., every two weeks, or monthly). Remember . . . sending out payments on a timely basis = a more driven and motivated affiliate marketing team = increased sales!

What Will be Your Mode of Payment?

Thanks to Paypal.com, making payments is an absolute breeze. Simply register for a business account and you're good to go. However, some of your affiliates might not be able to accept funds via Paypal. So it's a good idea to offer a wide variety of options including direct bank deposit, Skrill, Payoneer and check (via postal mail or DHL/FedEx).

Find Affiliates

The quickest way to do this is to join sites such as ShareASale, CommissionJunction, and ClickBank. These established and reputable affiliate networks already have a large pool of competent affiliates who are always on the lookout to promote high quality products and services. With this approach, you'll be heading towards your target, instead of hunting for it!

Create Effective Marketing Tools

Make it easy for affiliates to market your offers by creating a suite of marketing tools they can use. These can range from banners to ad copy to email messages.

Promote Your Affiliate Program

Have details about your affiliate scheme posted prominently on your website/blog. Explain what it's all about and state the many benefits people stand to gain when they become an affiliate for your business. In short, encourage them to sign up. All in all, an affiliate marketing scheme, if done right, can help your business grow to spectacular levels. That's why it's a strategy you may seriously want to consider implementing as soon as possible.

Create a Global Community

Establishing a global community (in other words, a loyal and responsive customer base across the world) brings plenty of benefits to a business including more exposure and brand recognition, more sales, and more profits. Which brings us to the question: what is the fastest and easiest way for a business to create a successful global community? The answer is: using and implementing powerful social media strategies.

In the past, interacting with international consumers on a constant basis was considered a challenge. Today, thanks to social media, it's a very straightforward process. Unfortunately though, the vast majority of businesses don't really capitalize on the benefits of this valuable tool, and often end up executing a poor strategy that brings less than stellar returns.

In the steps below, I outline two key lessons to keep in mind when carrying out a social media campaign to build your global community.

Lesson #1: Think Global, Go Local

Massively popular online networking sites such as Twitter, LinkedIn, and Facebook should not always be your "go-to" resources. Whether it's QZone in China or VK in Russia, by targeting social media platforms that locals in a country are most likely to use, you will successfully attract customers beyond the boundaries of the top three listed above.

Tip: Always make it a point to first research the local websites and observe how members interact with each other and what type and style of content best captures their interest.

Lesson #2: Zero in on Your Market

To put it another way, be market specific. Each and every market has its own set of unique characteristics, and while most of these are pretty obvious in theory, they can sometimes be overlooked when crafting a marketing strategy. For example, a red-hot, mid-summer advertising program aimed at the US market is bound to fall flat if it's released during the Brazilian winter, which usually occurs at the same time. That's why it pays to be on the ball when creating a promotional campaign for a specific market.

Additionally, seemingly "insignificant" things like colors and images should be taken into account and incorporated only if they are suited to your target audience; the last thing you want to do is offend potential customers and turn them off to your marketing message.

To conclude, it is certainly worth remembering that global communities are ultimately all about real human beings—with real feelings and emotions—and you should never lose sight of this in your quest to establish a global community through social media marketing.

Make the World Listen To You

According to the Chartered Institute of Marketing, the term "marketing" refers to the process used to identify, anticipate, and satisfy customer demands and requirements profitably.

An effective and well-rounded marketing strategy comprises two key components:

1. Online Marketing

2. Offline Marketing

For your business to thrive and succeed in the 21st century, you need component one. Ignore it and you're almost guaranteed to lose market share. After all, the Internet is arguably the most powerful medium of communication in history—and if you're not taking advantage of it, your competitors will.

With that said, dismissing component two would be foolish. Old-school tactics can still provide you with an edge over companies that focus exclusively on online marketing.

This leads us to our next question. What are some of the techniques you can use to market your business and stand out from the sea of competition?

Offline:

1. Join Your Local COC (Chamber of Commerce)

Actively taking part in local COC-related events can result in a big publicity boost for your company—and put you in touch with other like-minded professionals, some of whom will be interested in either purchasing your products/services or partnering with you on new, mutually beneficial projects.

2. Speak at Events/Workshops/Seminars

When you're running a business, it helps to position yourself and your company as the foremost authority in your target market. And one great way of doing this is to speak at various events and functions that provide you with a platform to really bring home this message. What's more, not only will you have members of the audience expressing interest in what you have to offer, there might also be prominent journalists/bloggers who, if they like what you're saying, will promote you in their publications/blogs.

Online:

1. Go Mobile

According to recent research, over 1.2 billion people access the Internet from their mobile phones, which means the chances of someone visiting your company website through a mobile device is pretty high. Furthermore, in a study released by Google, 61 percent of prospects have a more positive opinion of a brand when it offers a satisfying mobile experience. So how do you capture this particular market? By ensuring your site is mobile-optimized and investing in mobile advertising. You'll find it pays off massively.

2. Social Media Marketing

This form of marketing will play an even bigger role in the future. Companies are increasingly incorporating social media into their advertising campaigns because:

- It enables them to broadcast messages to their target market with a few simple clicks of the mouse.

- It helps keep customers engaged.

- It allows for an intimate relationship between a business and a consumer.

Bottom line—if used correctly, social media is a brilliant conversational marketing tool that can catapult your brand into a whole new level.

Alberto's Special Offer:

Ready to Take Your Business to the Next Level?
I'd like to talk about your business with you.

I'm doing thirty *free Strategy Sessions,* where we can talk about *your* business. You and I will create your very own *Business and Marketing Plan* to attract more clients and increase your sales powerfully for profitable results. It's your time to *shine* and make a *quantum leap* in *your* business and *your* life.

I've only got thirty places. Go and act...fast!

Call me—Alberto Liberal—directly at: 0034 682290700
Email me at: alberto@connectingyouglobally.com

About Alberto Liberal

Alberto Liberal has a solid record for outstanding productivity as a Controller, with more than a decade of experience producing accurate financial and management reports with improvement recommendations to top management.

With a degree in Economics, and a master's degree in Auditing and Management Control, plus extensive training in seminars for working professionals in finance, Alberto is a dynamic leader and team builder, who consistently motivates others toward success. He backs his mentoring with an intense love of learning, exceptional communication and problem-solving skills, and contageous enthusiasm to succeed. With an attitude for excellence, he puts every part of himself into achieving it. Connect with Alberto Liberal online and through social media:

Skype: albertoliberal

Facebook: http://www.Facebook/albertoliberalIM

Twitter: http://www.Twitter.com/albertoliberal

LinkedIn: http://www.LinkedIn.com/in/albertoliberal

**To find out more about Alberto, visit:
http://www.ConnectingYouGlobally.com**

Chapter 9

Networking Mastery
by Sam Rafoss, RHN

Networking is a critical skill you need to master to grow your personal brand and for the growth and expansion of your business.

I wasn't always the best at networking. When I attended my first networking group in 2004, I remember walking into the hotel and hearing a "buzz" that kept getting louder as I approached the meeting room. It reminded me of the buzzing of our honey bees on the farm where I grew up.

My first instinct was to turn around and run. Run . . . as fast as I could to my car, and drive back home to the comfort of my home, husband, and babies waiting for me. You see, I'm comfortable in front of a room, teaching, training, and presenting, but I'm truly not that comfortable in a room of socializing or networking.

I started my small business in 2002 after my second daughter was born. I wanted to be a stay-at-home mom, raise my girls, and still work because I loved it, and I wanted to make some money. I used my background in social work, marketing, training, and facilitating to offer parenting and self-esteem workshops. This allowed me to work around the girls' schedules. After two years, I realized I had exhausted all of my current work avenues and contacts, and needed to network to grow my business.

Even thought the "buzzing" terrified me, I knew I had to face the fear and just do it. I walked into the room with a smile on my face and introduced myself to the first woman I met, and so began my journey into the art of networking.

For some, networking is a breeze, and for others (like me at the start) it is torture. It involves putting yourself out there, letting others get to know you, and then waiting for the reaction. It is this varied reaction that causes people to shy away from networking. It helps to remember that others are feeling the same way. Networking simply involves meeting and interacting with others to attract people to your business, products, and services, and for people to get to know, like, and trust you and your business.

It was hard to leave the comfort of my home, but getting out from behind my computer and going to events in my field was one of the best decisions I've made. Relationships through networking have led to new and reoccurring business time and time again.

Step away from your comfort zone and attend workshops, seminars, and shows in your field. While you are at these events, make the most of your time. Even when you're at an event not necessarily related to your industry, you would be surprised at who you can meet.

Have a plan before you go into the event. I decide if I'm going to concentrate on generating clients or if the event is more suited to joint venture relationship building. It may end up being both, but having a goal helps keep me focused.

I also like to take the length of the event and determine who I would like to meet and how much time I can dedicate to the individual. But be careful not to make it mechanical either. Networking is relationship based, so you need to treat it as such. I've seen too many people come in to an event and start handing out cards or information as they "assault" you with their pitch of how they can help you, without even hearing what you need.

With that being stated, I've been to hundreds of events over the years, learned a lot, and have come up with my successful networking strategy.

I'll share my five-step strategy and then some bonus tips at the end, so you'll know how to network like a pro!

So let's take a look at the five steps to networking success:

1. The Initial Greeting and Interaction

2. Your Goal for Each Person You Meet

3. How to Become a Networking Butterfly

4. How to Follow Up

5. Nourish Relationships for Growth and Expansion

1. The Initial Greeting and Interaction

Smile as you first enter the room, and when you meet someone, remember they are just like you. They are there to meet people, get contacts, and grow their business, and you are just as good a prospect to them as they are to you. Be confident and have good eye contact and a firm handshake (notice if people wear lots of rings, don't squeeze too hard—it hurts). Introduce yourself, ask them what they do, and listen while they talk. Make note of what you can do to serve them and then you can see where you fit into what they do. When you listen as they talk first, you have the advantage of tailoring the conversation to what you can provide for them. When you talk about what you do, make it about them and how you can help them. Be yourself and get passionate about what you can do for them. People are drawn to confident leaders. Leave them with a lasting impression.

2. Your Goal for Each Person You Meet

Because *you* were the one who started the conversation, you gained the advantage of hearing about them first so, you can now speak to their needs. This also gives you time to think about your goal for each person you meet. I like to think win-win. How can we help each other? Could this person benefit from my services by becoming a client? Or, is this person better suited for a potential partnership or collaboration? Are they a great marketing contact? Whatever the person does, they can likely help you in some way. Even if it isn't for the purpose you approached them for, don't discount people. Whether you can help each other directly or indirectly, you never know who knows who. Be flexible, and keep each person in mind for something, and intend for the same in return. They may not need you, but if you've left a good impression, they're more likely to refer you to someone else who may need you. The win-win philosophy and mindset has proven to serve me well, and it's my wish for you, too.

3. How to Become a Networking Butterfly

Time is money when you are at a networking or social event. Once you have exchanged cards and information, and you have determined what the goal for this person is, it's time to move on. You need to respectfully and politely depart to meet someone else. The key is in the follow up after the event. That's when you decide who you'd like to meet for tea or coffee, where you can spend more time talking, but right now you have a mission. That mission is to meet as many people as possible in the time allocated. The relationship building and nurturing comes later. You can glance around and pre-select the next person who seems available, then thank your current prospect for their time. Make good eye contact again, tell them it was a pleasure meeting them (and you'll contact them next week), give a firm handshake, and move to your next person. Don't worry about leaving them alone. You are here to work the room and make your contacts. Remember, people are drawn to leaders. Even if you don't have time to personally meet everyone in the room, others may seek you out as someone worth getting to know. People take note of the "movers and shakers" and want to be a part of that group.

4. How to Follow Up

This is the time now where you take all of your business cards and information from the event, and get organized. Do this first thing when you return to your office. Know who was good for what (client, collaboration, marketing, joint venture). Sort them in a database such as Outlook, or simply email them and invite them to opt-in to your autoresponder system by letting them know about your free report or gift. Then plan your strategy for staying connected to them. If they were possible clients, call these people first. If you're nervous to call, have a scripted message and practice beforehand. Rehearsing will help you make sure your goal is met when you do make the call. Have another rehearsed script in case you get voice mail, but don't read it verbatim. Sound comfortable but don't ramble either. Leave your message and repeat your number at the end so it's easy for them to jot down without having to replay your message. Then keep working through your list, making sure to connect with everyone for your intended purpose. Remember, follow-up is just like the networking event itself—you have a lot of calls to make, so once you take the next action step, it's time to move on.

5. Nourish Relationships for Growth and Expansion

To reiterate, networking is about relationships with people, and if you are aware of personality styles, you know that people interact differently. Some make fast decisions and others take longer to engage with you or in your services. Notice how people interact with you and the language they use. If they say something like *"What's the bottom line?"* then this type of person usually tends to move quickly. Whereas, another may say *"I would like to work with someone who can take the time to help me . . . "* which is indicative they need more time and proof of how you can solve their problem. By listening to their words and noticing their behavior, and providing solutions geared to the individual, you are more likely to get your needs met too. Networking is a vital part of your growth and expansion, whether you do it at a live event or set up a strategy where you can do it online. Make sure you take care of all the people you meet. Keep in touch through newsletters, calls, and emails. Another favorite strategy of mine is to send cards by snail mail. Handwritten cards are a nice touch to remind people you are thinking of them, and they stand out from the bills and junk mail. Be genuine, honest, and nurturing to these relationships no matter what methods you use. It will make a significant contribution to your business.

This is my overall five-step strategy for networking. Over the years, my business has evolved from parenting classes, to becoming a registered holistic nutritionist (RHN) and teaching in the health and wellness field, to speaking, coaching, and mentoring holistic entrepreneurs. I started doing this because I found the same fears and problems for this market. Holistic practitioners are a talented group of amazing gifted healers, but are not typically good at the business and marketing of their business—which is the part I love. So when my students and colleagues began seeking my advice I was hooked into learning more in order to teach and share more. Here are seven more tips I've discovered.

7 *Bonus* Networking Tips!

1. Be clear about what your message is before heading to a networking event. People do not want to be rude, but they also do not have time to listen to a lengthy explanation of what you do. The time for that is at a follow-up meeting.

2. Make sure your business card is professionally done and easy to read. Include your headshot on your card to make it easy for people to remember you. Do not hand out your card if the person has not asked for it.

3. Respect the guidelines of networking groups. If it is your first time to a group, ask the leader or a member what the rules and processes of the group are.

4. Even if they gave you their card, never automatically add anyone to your email list (autoresponder system). Send a separate email to remind them of how you met, and to

invite them to join your community or get a free gift, or to let them know how to keep in touch.

5. If you attend networking events as a business, you need a website. Preferably a landing page or website you host, with an opt-in feature to capture emails to build your contact list.

6. Even if you have a base of clients and referrals, if you are networking, these contacts will search online for you to review you and your business. Here are some recent statistics:

- 78 percent of Internet users conduct product research online (Hubspot 2011).

- 69 percent of web users trust online reviews as much as they trust personal recommendations.

- 96 percent of Internet users have used a search engine to research professional services.

- 80 percent of consumers rank search engines as the most useful tool when making a buying decision (Local Consumer Review 2013).

7. Bottom line—for networking to work for you to grow and build your business, you have to be online. Take a look around at every networking meeting. People are on their smart phones "Googling" websites or your name, posting to Facebook, Pinterest, or Instagram, and tweeting to their followers.

Successful networking to nourish your relationships with the goal of growing and expanding your business takes place offline and online. Follow the five-step process and take note of the seven bonus tips, and you'll be a networking pro in no time.

Sam Rafoss
Business Strategist for Nutrition and Holistic Practices

Sam's Special Offer:

Bonus #1: Get Your Copy of
***The Four Fundamentals
to a Booming Holistic Business***
at http://www.MakingMoneyasaNutritionist.com

Bonus #2: If you check yes to both options,
then contact me for your free strategy call.

Yes! ☐ I am a holistic entrepreneur and would love to learn how to boom my business.

Yes! ☐ I have purchased a copy of *Start Right Marketing*.

Email your receipt for *Start Right Marketing* to sam@samrafoss.com and I will schedule a fifteen-minute strategy call with you to discuss how I can help you attract your ideal clients so you can make more money and boom your business.

About Sam Rafoss

Sam Rafoss, RHN, is from Canada and is a speaker, author, and a business & marketing strategist for nutrition and holistic practices.

Sam is a contributing author in the bestselling Adventures in Manifesting Series—*Conscious Business: 33 Stories to Ignite Your Entrepreneurial Spirit*. She is a member of CAPS (Canadian Association of Professional Speakers) Calgary, has diplomas in Social Work and Natural Nutrition, and is a Registered Karuna Reiki Master. Sam understands first-hand how gifted healers struggle with marketing themselves and their services.

As a healer and a marketer, Sam has made it her mission to share her unique combination of spiritual and holistic marketing expertise to help the healers of the world attract their ideal clients and make money doing what they love to do.

A recipient of the 2014 Amazing Coach Award from the Inspirational Business Leaders Council, Sam is serving her higher purpose so others can serve theirs.

When you're ready to boom your business, Sam takes you by the hand and ensures you create the life of your dreams.

To find out more about Sam, visit:
http://www.SamRafoss.com

Chapter 10

Increase Your Reach through Internet Radio, Web TV, and Live Events
by Nadine Lajoie

How would you like to get more exposure for your business and your services? Would you like to have more leads and increase your conversion rate? For sure, traditional media exposure can help tremendously with that, but not everyone can get this opportunity right away. First, they need to build their credibility, expert status, and recognition.

Becoming an expert in your industry is not always easy but nowadays, there are so many tools we can use through the Internet, anyone can have their message heard and shared all over the world. At the same time, you need to go over the top and "scream" louder if you want to get heard by the traditional media, social media, the Internet, etc. So, I want to share with you three tools to help you increase your exposure, your leads, and your conversion rate.

Tool #1—Start Your Own Internet Radio Show

Did you know that 77 million Americans will listen to Internet radio streams on both computers and mobile devices by January 1, 2015 (see source next page*)? You cannot discount

Start Right Marketing

* www.noxsolutions.com/f/Internet-Radio#sthash.6hOCmCez.dpuf

anymore, especially since by doing your own show, you can be discovered by other Internet radio hosts or even get offers to be a guest on traditional radio shows once they discover you and your level of professionalism.

Creating your own Internet radio show is really easy, quick, and efficient, and you can do it within one hour and broadcast whenever you want, attracting listeners and new customers. Another advantage to hosting your own Internet radio show is that you'll be perfecting your craft, becoming really natural and organized in your thoughts by practicing over and over again, thus making it easier for you to get booked with traditional radio and TV.

You can create your Internet radio show for *free* by going to http://www.programyourlife.org. You can also access a free trial at http://www.WomensRadio.com (it is $19.95 a month for the software after the trial period). In addition, there are many other Internet radio programs online that may charge you somewhere around $39 to few hundred dollars a month, and some claim they can even help you get sponsors. The use of podcasts and programs like iTunes can also serve as free solutions.

Now that you have a platform, you need to decide on your template. Later, we'll discuss that and the target customers you want to attract. Once you have these elements—*bingo*—you are ready to go!

To record your radio show, you will need two types of software, a telephone (preferably a land-line), and a three-way conference option directly from your phone, which will give you better quality audio than if you register for a three-way conference line service.

I mentioned that you need two types of software. The first is Audio Acrobat (http://nlajoie.audioacrobat.com), which can be downloaded. With this software, you can record new audio, and easily create and/or upload your mp3s. Next, as the radio show producer, you will need software to edit those radio interviews (if you want to), as well as to add introduction music, announcements, a theme song, sponsors, commercial breaks, an ending template for your show, etc. You can decide what you want to do. Let your creativity go, and spread the message you are meant to spread around the world.

Audacity is free editing software you can download from the Internet, and it is easy to use (http://audacity.sourceforge.net). You can do everything you need to with it, such as fade-in, fade-out, generate silence, make transitions, reduce noise, etc.

As an example of how easy it is to set up your Internet radio show, here's a quick story. I told one of my coaches that I would start my radio show by a certain date, and at 2:00 a.m. on that date I realized I had not yet done it. I quickly got busy, and I was able to build my own radio show between 2:00 a.m. and 5:00 a.m. (I'm a night owl)! By 7:00 a.m. that morning, it was on the Internet. If I could do it from scratch, so can you—in less than one hour—with my step-by-step process, *Radio Guide 101* (http://www.keepdreamingkeepliving.org/pages/radio-guide).

Three things I suggest you get from your guests, that will save you a lot of time and stress, especially at the beginning, are:

1. A Press Kit (including bio and picture)

2. A Questions & Topic Sheet (or bullet points of their topic)

3. A Release Contract (so you can reuse the interview *)

*Note: *You can build your CD series of experts for less than two dollars a CD (http://www.Kunaki.com), with no minimum required, and they can even ship for you, so there's no inventory to manage! What a great way to create products with other's people knowledge and credibility!*

You also prepare for your guests—in advance—a specific email which you ask them to promote to their email list, as well as a "blurb" or two (that you write for them), along with your link, that they can use to let their social media friends and contacts know about their spot on your show. This will expose you to their followers and will help you tremendously to increase your reach and attract more customers to you.

If you are an expert, a speaker, a coach, or any kind of leader, this is the easiest and fastest way to be recognized as an expert, because you invite other experts in your industry to be on your show. This also helps you build relationships with the people you want to be associated with. Mostly, those experts will say yes to you, giving them a medium to spread *their* message, and you are more likely to get invited onto *their* stage, radio show, or TV show. First giving them the opportunity to get exposure will surely get you on the good side of the fence. People will see you differently and when you go to networking events, you will set yourself apart and raise your own credibility. That is what happened to me, and I really encourage you to do the same. Like it has been for books, radio shows are the new trend and your "new business card."

Tool #2—Start Your Own Web TV Show

The Web TV show elevates you one step further into the media realm, because now people can see you on camera, like on TV. People are watching their movies and TV shows on their computers, and one click later, they can see you on your Web TV or YouTube channel. It is up to you to show up in a bigger way and look as professional as you can. You can even set up your web studio for around $300, so please don't tell me you cannot do it!

Google Hangouts is doing a fantastic job, and so I chose to do mine with them, because it is free, easy, and when you finish your show, it downloads directly to your YouTube Channel and broadcasts immediately. How much easier than that can it be?

For show success, you need solid content, credible guests, riveting topics, a great template to organize your thoughts (http://www.keepdreamingkeepliving.org/pages/bronze), and you and your guests must promote your show through social media. The more you do that—consistently, repetitively, and in a professional manner—the more people will notice you, trust you, give you business, and pay more for your services.

Everything is a matter of perception, and please don't hide your head in the sand. If someone wants to hire you, they will visit your website, Google your name, and look at your Facebook account, right? Go ahead and Google your name and mine too! I came to the United States in December of 2007. I knew nobody here, barely spoke English, and still had a strong French Canadian accent, so everybody told me I would never make it! Well, I did, and so can you! I spoke on big stages with top speakers in the country, was listened to by over ten million listeners on national radio and TV Shows, and now I have my "RACING to Success Minute" daily broadcasts to over three million people—not so bad for someone who was not supposed to make it!

Think outside the box and create your own feel, your own signature, and your own branding. This is why it is so important to have the right coaches and mentors around you who really made it for themselves. Still, *you* have to do the work to make things happen. Do whatever you can control, without waiting for the media to discover you. You have no more excuses to continue procrastinating, unless you still think you can stay at home or at your office and attract all the customers, abundance, and freedom you desire.

Tool #3—Build Your Own Live Events

In my opinion, live events with too many speakers, lectures, boring presentations, or "pitch festivals" are over—since a few years ago—so you need to be creative and become experiential. If you really want to transform people's lives from the inside out, touch their hearts and heal their souls, and make the planet a better place, your events need to be *transactional* and *transformational* at the same time. Include different teachings, lessons, processes, tools, and strategies; but also bring hands-on elements, exercises, and small group sharing, so people can integrate and work on their own businesses or personal growth, right on the spot. We all know that motivation is really cool when you go to a seminar, but too often, people go back the very next day to their old routines. This is why it's so important to add the transformational portion to our events.

Find an angle and something different you can offer that goes with your branding and your message. Bring in sponsors and experts to add credibility, too. As an example, I'm the founder of the "World Premiere Leadership Trainings at the Racetrack" (http://www.NadineRacing.com/workshop), for businesses and entrepreneurs, and one of the transformational breakthrough exercises we offer is that people can go on a tandem ride with a professional racer, up to 150 mph! With Tony Robbins, they walk on the fire, but with Nadine, they go on a bike for eight to ten minutes! I know you think this is pretty cool and unique, and that this is easy for me, but for three years, I fought with my coaches, mentors, friends, and colleagues because everybody told me that was too crazy, dangerous, and not realizable. Again, find something outside the box for you. Be stubborn and do whatever it takes to make it happen!

Here's a tool called "The Expert Grid Blueprint™" that I developed from all of the coaching I received for my speaking, media appearances, and coaching business. It will help you become efficient. It features nine critical components to build each section of your events and your media interviews quickly: http://www.keepdreamingkeepliving.org/pages/bronze. The 9 critical components of the blueprint include:

1. Story

2. Lesson

3. Songs/Music

4. Hook

5. Credibility

6. Problem

7. Solution

8. Tool

9. Exercises

Once you build your "Expert Grid Blueprint™" for each of your stories or lessons you want to teach, it's easy to plug and play and react quickly when something happens during your event or your interview. Instead of being unbalanced and destabilized, you remain calm and in control of the situation. You can breathe—even if you have to race at 180 mph in your head, like on a motorcycle racetrack—because you know exactly what to say, whether it's for a three-minute interview or a seven-day retreat.

You can add more content or pictures or stories for each of your lessons, and invite different experts to cover—or complete and reinforce—the point you want to make.

The blueprint is also helpful when you prepare your guest's questions or interviews after you get their info. Use it with just a few words, so you can have an overview before the interview. Or, when you interview your guest, take some notes directly onto your blueprint, and tie it with one or your lessons, so the conversation goes smoothly and naturally between you and your guest.

There are many new ways to do business and to increase your exposure, and I don't want you to be left out, so take the wave while it is still near the beginning. Position yourself as an expert in your industry, and build your different products and your platform to gain credibility. Work on your message and your template, download your "Expert Grid Blueprint™," and get your video training on http://www.NadineCoaching.com.

Please let me know how I can be your mentor. Call me at 949-421-7562 to schedule your appointment. I hope to help you soon on your R.A.C.I.N.G. Journey to SUCCESS, at 180 mph!

Increase Your Reach through Internet Radio, Web TV, and Live Events

Nadine's Special Offer:

Bonus #1: Create your own Internet radio show with Nadine's ***Radio Guide 101***
Get your copy at:
http://www.KeepDreamingKeepLiving.org/pages/radio-guide

Bonus #2: A 30-minute ***Complimentary Strategy Session*** with Nadine

To become an expert in your industry and learn how to:

- Build your credibility as an expert with more media exposure

- Develop the 9 components of your "Expert Grid BlueprintTM"

- Attract more business by creating your own internet radio/web TV show

- Create your *6-Step Action Plan* with Nadine's ***Prosperity R.A.C.I.N.G. SystemTM***

Please be sure to register and download over $2,000 in extra gifts for you at **http://www.NadineCoaching.com**

About Nadine Lajoie

Nadine Lajoie (pronounced lage-wah) is an international award-winning Entrepreneur, Speaker, and America's High Speed Success Coach.

Retired and a millionaire at age 41, she also became a "Champion Motorcycle Racer who Sings like an Angel."

Nadine is a radio host, co-founder of "Teen CEO Reality TV Show," and the founder of "R.A.C.I.N.G. to SUCCESS™," the "World Premiere Leadership Training at the Racetrack." She is training and "IN-Powering" entrepreneurs worldwide to achieve high performance, ACCELERATE success, build systems, and increase productivity and credibility.

Nadine Lajoie has been in News outlets such as Forbes, USA Today, ABC, FOX, and CBS Money Watch, and has been featured in magazines, on TV and radio, and on stages around the world, along with personalities and speakers including: Oprah Winfrey, Donald Trump, Zig Ziglar, Jamie Lee Curtis, Les Brown, Marianne Williamson, Michael B. Beckwith, Adam Markel, and Tom Hopkins. She is a #1 best-selling author of *Win The Race of Life* (four time book award finalist, USA/London), and co-author with Les Brown in *Fight for Your Dreams*.

To find out more about Nadine, visit: http://www.NadineRacing.com

Chapter 11

Growing Your Influence and Impact to Epidemic Levels
by Teresa de Grosbois

The valley is on fire. Grey smoke billows to the southeast. The noise is deafening, a crackling roar louder than I can shout. Fire leaps hundreds of feet into the air as dry white pine needles snap in the heat. Jack pinecones, ignited by the wildfire, burst apart like fireworks, sending burning embers and pine seeds high in the air. The strong winds carry the flaming detritus downwind, sometimes for miles, where they land in the dry pine needles and start new spot fires that grow and join together, forming the advancing edge of the wildfire.

In spite of the turmoil around me and the unpredictability of wildfires, I feel safe. Between me and the wildfire are hundreds of exhausted and soot-covered firefighters, and millions of dollars worth of fire-fighting equipment, but most importantly, I'm upwind. This wildfire is fueled and steered by the wind, and right now it's headed away from me.

It's the summer between my sophomore and junior years in high-school and I'm earning college money by delivering groceries to firefighters in the woods near where I grew up in northern Canada. Being this close to such a destructive force is sobering for me. A wildfire is a massive force of change, releasing an almost unfathomable amount of energy that leads ultimately to new growth.

I can think of no better metaphor than a wildfire to illustrate how word-of-mouth spreads. Word-of-mouth epidemics are both predictable and surprising in the same moment. You can plan them, even control them, but they can also take on a life of their own.

Starting a word-of-mouth epidemic requires a level of inner steeliness—a willingness to fuel a force of nature that might grow beyond your control. If you have a mission in life, if you feel you were put here for a reason, then make that your steel, because massive influence, brings massive impact.

Fame and Influence

Pop Quiz

You want to take a vacation from your business. You:

a) Book the plane tickets and go. Your business can run without you.

b) Start planning to inform your customers you'll be shut down for a week.

c) Vacation? What's that?

First let's think about what fame and influence might do for you. When you work with your customers and clients one at a time, you're probably finding them one at a time. Maybe your colleague recommends someone, or maybe you meet someone at a networking function. If you deal with your customers one at a time, you're essentially trading your hours for dollars. In

Growing Your Influence and Impact to Epidemic Levels

the business world we call that being self-employed. You don't really have a true business that keeps running if you walk away.

When you start reaching your clients in groups, you're no longer trading your hours for dollars. You're moving into the realm of influence. In the context used in this discussion, influence is distinct from fame. Fame is having many people know you, influence is having many people know, like, and trust you. When you speak, they act. Fame personified is Kim Kardashian and Brittney Spears, while those who best represent influence would be Gandhi or Martin Luther King.

Think about fame for a moment.

"He is an overnight sensation."

You often hear this term in the media. But if you look more closely you see years leading up to the "overnight" and probably a long trail of hard work and important steps.

The athlete who makes the big leagues, the author who suddenly finds themselves on The New York Times bestseller list, the expert who makes it onto Oprah—each of them traveled a path that led them to where they arrived. When you look, you'll see there are common elements in each path.

Every word-of-mouth epidemic acts a lot like a wildfire. You can predict it, even plan it, yet it will surprise you, maybe even overwhelm you, in the same moment. Hang around fire rangers long enough and you'll learn that every wildfire needs three elements to thrive:

- A spark to ignite
- Fuel to burn
- Wind to spread

Absent of any one of these elements, there is no wildfire. Similarly, every word-of-mouth epidemic needs three elements to take off.

Spark

What's your problem? Seriously, what problem do you solve for others?

Every word-of-mouth epidemic has at the heart of it the solution to a really great problem. That's the spark. A big spark catches easy: big problem, big epidemic.

Many new business owners who come to me for coaching fall short on this one. They are trying to solve everything for everyone, unwilling to pick one problem and truly stand for its solution.

It's hard to see the snake oil salesman when they are standing in the mirror. If what you're selling is not clearly targeted at some problem, that is how you appear to others: like someone who thinks they have the miraculous cure to everything. With no targeted evidence for solving a specific problem, you likely appear under-qualified, weak, and ingenuous.

Pop Quiz

What's your inner dialogue? Select all that apply:

a) I don't want to risk loosing any customers, so I won't focus on a specific thing.

b) I'm not ready to do my dream. My dream is big, therefore it must be hard.

Growing Your Influence and Impact to Epidemic Levels

c) I'll just do this "quick-win idea" to make money, then I'll go after something challenging.

Think about it. Do you want to buy something you don't really need from someone who doesn't really inspire you because they're "just practicing at business"?

The understood rulebook around this is, "*You must solve a clearly identifiable problem that people care about—the bigger, the better.*"

Mahatma Gandhi, Martin Luther King Jr., Nelson Mandela, all became globally significant because they stood courageously on the biggest problem going on throughout the planet at the time. Each of them would have described themselves as an inadequate leader. But they stood for the solution to human equality so courageously, that followers flocked to them. Their mistakes and missteps became irrelevant. The problem they tackled was so great it did not matter if what they did was perfect.

If you're a nutritionist, you may be solving the problem of how to loose weight. An even more specific, and therefore bigger problem, would be how someone can keep from getting sick by avoiding gluten or dairy products. With a work of fiction, a writer seeks to help people live a more exciting, fulfilled life. Add to that a moral lesson you stand for and you become even more specific. A self-help writer might tackle the problem of not enough money.

The more specific and bigger the problem, the more likely people will buy it. In other words, do something people really care about. It's much easier to create a wildfire epidemic around your work if it's something people deeply resonate with and can connect to in their own lives.

Martin Luther King Jr., Mahatma Gandhi, and Nelson Mandela are all great demonstrations of this. An even more important characteristic each man shared was their passion for their cause . . . which leads us to the fuel in the wildfire.

Fuel

"I have dream."

Read those words, and you immediately know I'm quoting Dr. Martin Luther King Jr. from one of the most studied and quoted speeches in global history. Newspapers and television media around the world covered that important occasion.

Yet few people remember the first words of that speech. On a whim, I asked several friends, both American and Canadian what they think the first words of that speech were. Half cannot even venture a guess. Two guess *"Four score years ago . . ."* one guesses *"Five score years ago . . ."* (which is accurately the second statement of the speech) and one, who is a history buff, accurately quotes *"I am happy to join with you today, in what will go down in history as the greatest demonstration for freedom in the history of our nation."*

Search on YouTube for "Martin Luther King I have a dream" and watch that speech. You will notice something most people miss, including many of the historians and communications experts that have written long essays on that speech. For the first eleven minutes of the speech, Dr. King reads purposefully and expertly from his notes. His words are carefully designed and delivered to paint a clear picture, a clear call-to-action. Three times he makes a call-to-action saying, *"Now is the time!"* and he repeatedly calls for peaceful and respectful resistance. Then at just past eleven minutes, something magical happens. Dr. King stops looking at his notes. His emotional energy shifts. Every cell of his being speaks his passion and he begins to speak entirely from the heart. There

Growing Your Influence and Impact to Epidemic Levels

is no longer a glance at a script in front of him, just words spoken from the heart. His passion is so great that housewives across the world talk about this being the moment they stopped working in the kitchen and walked over to the television set.

"*So even though we still face the difficulties of today and tomorrow, I still have a dream. It is a dream deeply rooted in the American dream. I have a dream that one day this nation will rise up and live out the true meaning of its creed.*"

King uses the phrase "*I have a dream*" seven more times before the end of the speech. Each sentence produces a vivid image of a reality that is right in front of us for the taking. An image rooted in passion and belief.

The "fuel" in the wildfire is how passionate you are in what you do. Passion sells. The greater passion level, the more engaging you are. People are drawn to passion.

As well, the greater the passion, the more likely you'll get interviews in all forms of media. Shawne Duperon talks about the "peeling carrots test." If you were on TV, would someone stop peeling carrots at the sink to come over and watch you? If so, you know your passion is at the right level.

Pop Quiz

Which of the following most accurately describes you?

a) You live to work. You so love what you do that you'll never retire.

b) You work to live, you can't wait to retire some day.

c) Shoot me now. I can't stand the thought of doing this another day.

Being passionate about what you do is a big part of authenticity. Authenticity is frequently talked about these days, though few people define it. Here's my definition: authenticity is your inner voice saying the same thing as your outer voice.

You can spot a phony a mile away. So if your mind is saying *"Oh God, I need this sale"* and your outer voice is saying *"this is a really great product, you should try it,"* everyone can spot you for the phony you are. That's primarily what *"The Law of Attraction"* is. If your emotional state is positive and passionate, people are drawn to you and want to help you. If inwardly you're focused on your own pain, boredom, or fear, people are not drawn to you. In fact they may even be repelled.

If you don't passionately love what you do, you have two choices:

1. Find a way to connect with why you love it, or

2. Change what you're doing.

Wind

"All I was doing was trying to get home from work" was one of the more famous statements of Rosa Parks when speaking about the 1955 December incident in Montgomery, Alabama, where she was arrested and put on trial for refusing to move to the back of the bus.

Rosa Parks' case became the rally point of the Montgomery Bus Boycott, which became the focal point of the civil rights movement in the United States. A then relatively unknown Baptist minister rallied the movement to the level of global significance. What was it that transformed a 28 year-old man fresh out of Bible College into a global icon?

Growing Your Influence and Impact to Epidemic Levels

There were several factors in that recipe. Not the least of which were purpose and passion, which we've already discussed. But let's not overlook the obvious. Martin Luther King Jr. gave influence to Rosa Parks. It's a fundamental principle of influence.

Just like if you want respect, you give respect. If you want influence, you give influence. More importantly, you give influence to someone who's truly congruent with who you are, so you can authentically talk about your respect for them.

Leaders of the civil rights movement in Montgomery had looked at a similar case eight months prior. In March 1955, a fifteen year-old schoolgirl in Montgomery, Claudette Colvin, refused to give up her bus seat. King was on the committee from the Birmingham African-American community that looked into the case. Colvin was pregnant and unmarried, so E.D. Nixon and Clifford Durr decided to wait for a better case to get behind. They shrewdly decided to not put the reigns of a civil rights movement into the hands of a terrified fifteen-year-old girl.

One of the most important acts King did that led to his global stature, was to be Rosa Parks' first raving fan. He showed her leadership and courage to the world and credited her with the leader she was already becoming in the civil rights movement. From that act, King's leadership and courage solidified.

Choose to whom you give influence and give it abundantly. It will define you as an influencer. The "wind" in the wildfire is your relationship with all those people you need to have talking about you or what you stand for.

When you have strong relationships with other influencers you can make mistakes everywhere and it won't matter. People who love you will catch every ball you drop.

It was two weeks before US Thanksgiving when Debbi Dachinger calls me. *"I've declared I'm going to be a bestselling author this year!"* Her enthusiasm leaps through the phone. I smile at her naiveté, declaring that putting together a bestseller campaign in a month or days boarders on insanity, let alone running one in the Christmas buying season, when competition is fierce. I tell her this. I quote the expression, *"It takes nine months to deliver a baby, no matter how many women you assign."* An aggressive campaign would be three months. I can't imagine pulling one off in a month. She'd have to get her book published in record time.

She hangs up the phone and meditates on the question. Every message she is getting is to "throw it to the angels and move forward." In the coming week she moves mountains and works tirelessly to publish the book.

On our second phone call, she is adamant. *"Sometimes you just have to declare something to the Universe and it will happen,"* she says. Debbi teaches law of attraction principles and goal setting on her radio show, *Dare to Dream*. She lives and breathes everything she teaches.

Then something magical happens. As she talks more about her plans, her belief enrolls me in the possibility of doing the impossible. I catch the miracle she is creating.

"Well Debbi, one of things I teach is that wildfires are unpredictable. There is magic in wildfires. People who are deeply inspired by you and what you stand for will sometimes crawl through glass to see you succeed. There is one thing I know Debbi—many people deeply love you." I laugh in shock as Debbi infects me with her own belief.

Dare to Dream is internationally syndicated, and heard by millions every week around the globe. More importantly, Debbi has helped thousands of thought-leaders get their work out to the masses. Debbi is a radio host who brings the best out

Growing Your Influence and Impact to Epidemic Levels

of everyone. She also is a founding member of the Evolutionary Business Council and beloved in that community. They are thought-leaders from around the world who are committed to helping other thought-leaders teach the principle of success.

I'm enrolled in throwing caution to the wind. Debbi gets on the phone and starts calling the people who love her and can help. Her passion is tireless. This book will help thousands. That is her fuel. Debbi speaks to them from her passion. Like me they are enrolled in helping. Everyone is a yes to talking about the book on Debbi's birthday.

Over the next week, I receive several calls from dozens of people wanting to help Debbi on her book launch. Dean Edelson, one of the top marketers in North America, even offers to re-write the emails Debbi is sending out to something more compelling. Others spread the word to other influencers to give her a hand.

Piece by piece, experts from every area fix what there is to be fixed and carry Debbi's campaign forward. Debbi's drive and passion has spread like wildfire. The buzz starts even before the book has launched. Influencers who know Debbi are rushing to come to the party. No one wants to be late.

By end of the week, Debbi is a bestseller in three categories; a remarkable feat during the Christmas buying season, not to mention her book has subsequently won two awards.

When the spark and the fuel are present as they are clearly with Debbi, then strong relationships are the wind in your wildfire. The influencers are the flaming pinecones that explode and expand your wildfire. People who love you want to see you succeed. That is the stuff miracles are made of.

The Rulebook

A lot of what I teach in my online programs is how you get into a relationship with other influencers. For this, you have to get past the gatekeepers and not show up as weird or someone who doesn't belong there.

In just about everything in life there is a rulebook for how a game is played. Every game has a known rulebook and an understood rulebook. In the game of hockey, the known rulebook is what happens on the rink—how the game is scored and refereed. The understood rulebook is what's expected of a player off the rink.

Everything that happens off the rink is largely related to the relationships that are required. If a player alienates his coach or insults the media, it's less likely he will progress to the higher leagues. Sometimes we call this politics, but the understood rulebook of any game is as important, if not more so, than the known rulebook.

The game of influence has an understood rulebook like any other. So let's talk dealing with the influential. What are the rules—known and understood?

A lot of people do the behavioral equivalent of standing in the middle of the hockey rink with a badminton racket and wonder why everyone's looking at them like they're weird, and not passing them the puck. There's an unspoken speech code and an unspoken etiquette in the influence game that you need to become conversant with.

First and foremost, you need to understand how to get into relationships with influencers. There are a number of mistakes people frequently make in this realm. Much of the content of my advanced programs online speaks to these. The biggest mistake is what I affectionately call the "premature ask."

Growing Your Influence and Impact to Epidemic Levels

Pop Quiz

There is someone influential you really want to meet. You:

a) Take a "don't ask, don't get" philosophy and assertively ask for help.

b) Offer to bake them cookies.

c) Are you crazy? I'd never approach someone influential.

The premature ask is the equivalent of when you move into a new house and the neighbor runs by and says, *"Hey, great lawn mower! Can't wait to borrow that baby."* You roll your eyes back in your head and think, *"Shoot me now. Who have I got for a neighbor?"* Have this go on long enough and you'll likely not answer the door when they come by.

Many people meet an influencer and fall into a mindset of *"Omigod! This is my one chance. I better go ask for what I need."*

You rush over to the influencer, get in line, wait 25 minutes for your chance, and then blurt out your "ask." You are shocked when the influencer rolls their eyes back in their head and gives their assistant a look of *"Shoot me now. Who is this?"*

In the same way, you don't want to answer the door for the obnoxious neighbor, the influencer's gatekeepers suddenly get in your way.

The first thing to do when you meet an influencer is offer them support. To put it metaphorically, you are bringing the new neighbor a plate of cookies or a vase of fresh flowers.

What does this look like? The currency of influence is influence. In other words, the most meaningful thing you can ever offer an influencer is more influence. In the influence game, that equals bringing the new neighbor cookies.

This is why you should have your own following, your own social media reach, and your own list. When you meet an influencer, you can say things like, *"Wow, I love what you talked about. Can I repost some of your content to my blog?"* or *"Can I interview you on my radio show?"* or *"I understand you're doing an event in New York next week. Maybe I can shout that out on my Facebook page or send that out to my Twitter following."*

That's the equivalent of bringing the flowers or cookies. It creates the energy of *"Let's have a collaborative energy between us. Let's be friends. Let's help each other."* Suddenly you find the gatekeepers are no longer barring your way.

The second biggest mistake you can make is to offer the wrong thing.

Pop Quiz

You meet an influencer and want to offer them something nice. You offer to:

a) Clean their house

b) Buy them lunch

c) Write about them in a blog post

OK, most of you thought offering to clean their house would be weird. But I know many of you chose "buy them lunch." The best answer is, in fact, c.

When you first learned marketing, you learned what the experts would call "referral marketing" and "networking." How

Growing Your Influence and Impact to Epidemic Levels

do you meet lots of leads, develop relationship, and end up with customers or clients? This is where the understood rulebook gets tricky.

One of the things you learned in networking is what to do when you meet someone important to you. You offer to buy them a coffee or lunch. It's the perfect thing to do, right? Consider this—if you met her, would you offer to buy Oprah Winfrey a coffee? Of course the answer is no. Not only would her gatekeepers get in the way, you might end up arrested for stalking.

Somewhere between "the lead you met at a networking function" and "Oprah," the understood rulebook changed. Somewhere, offering to buy someone a coffee became rude instead of polite. It became the wrong thing to offer.

That's because influential people deeply value their time. It's their most valuable commodity next to influence itself.

Get in Action

Knowing how to generate influence will make no difference to you until you develop habits of daily actions. Living your dreams lies in action. Otherwise you're just dreaming. Routinely gifting influence to other people is foundational to developing yourself as an influencer who has impact on the world.

Think about those things you can potentially offer to an influencer that might have meaning to them. One of the reasons to grow your social media, grow your newsletter following, or have a blog or radio show is to have lots of cool things to offer.

Start a meet up group at Meetup.com, start a teleseminar series, or host a major event. Any of these things can work in the influence world. Do whichever one is most aligned with your skills and most resonates with you.

One of the things I cover in my more advanced programs is the nuts and bolts of how you do some of these things—how you go from ground zero and work through the steps of becoming an influencer, one step at a time.

The reality is none of the steps are particularly difficult. You just need somebody to show you how. Are you interested in learning more? Come check out some of our advanced programs at WildfireAcademy.com

Here are ten actions you can offer an influencer to build your relationship (and all of these are easy for you to build and carry out):

1. Introduce them to another influential person.

2. Give a shout out of their event/work on your social media.

3. Repost their blog to your blog, with a link to their content.

4. Mention them in your newsletter.

5. Quote their work on your blog.

6. Write an article about them.

7. Mail your contacts on LinkedIn in a certain city that their event is coming to town (LinkedIn let's you sort your mailings by city).

8. Share the content from their Facebook page and talk about it on your page.

9. Interview them on your BlogTalkRadio show.

10. Invite them to speak at an event you host.

Growing Your Influence and Impact to Epidemic Levels

Wildfire Academy
Our Member Only On-line Training Site

Teresa's Special Offer:

*Igniting Wildfire Word-of-Mouth—
Going Flame to Fame in 30 Days*
Free 4-week program

Explore new trends, tools, and success stories to create a movement to make the world a better place, with daily 5-minute exercises to learn the influence game. Master:

-Using your passion to influence the way others think
-Developing the routine habits that create fame
-Leveraging your social media in powerful ways
-Creating big energy around your book, business, or project
-Moving from local word-of-mouth to wildfire epidemics

Sign up for the free 4-week program at:
http://www.WildfireAcademy.com/Free-gift

Also included: optional free subscription to Wildfire News. Teresa's bi-weekly newsletter of tips and recommendations.

About Teresa de Grosbois

Teresa de Grosbois is an International speaker, trainer and #1 international best-selling author. She has been featured in media across Canada and the US, including CBC, Global, CTV and City TV. She is passionate about teaching others to play bigger and generate wealth by creating more powerful relationships, both locally and internationally. She is an expert on growing influence and generating word-of-mouth. She teaches how to grow your profit or personal success by getting authentic and intentional about how you connect with people. In a world where paid advertising is becoming ineffective, Teresa teaches how to create and succeed with influence and word-of-mouth.

As the founder and chair of the Evolutionary Business Council, Teresa leads an international, invitation-only council of speakers and influencers who are focused on teaching principles of success. Teresa's extensive background in business includes leadership roles in several organizations.

Teresa is a big thinker and a big doer. An avid outdoor enthusiast, she has climbed Mount Kilimanjaro with her two daughters to raise money for schools in Africa. Teresa believes it is possible to eradicate poverty by changing the way people think. She arranges speaking tours into developing countries to teach business and empowerment skills to University students and small business owners.

To find out more about Teresa, visit:
http://www.WildfireAcademy.com

Chapter 12

Two Big Bangs for Your Influence-Marketing Buck: Publish a Book and a Digital Magazine
by Margo DeGange, M.Ed.

Being a content marketing specialist and book publisher, I love to see business owners embrace the option to lead others and gain influence though the writing and distribution of solid, high-quality, desirable, content—content that is engaging, informative, interesting, relevant, and reliable. Why just be a "marketer" when you can become an "Influence Marketer"?

As a business owner and brand, you have the enormous and exciting opportunity to help build, shape, influence, and persuade your community by providing them with great content. I call this brand engagement!

This book is about *starting right* in your marketing efforts, and continuing on the *right* path to growth going forward. Your sales and profits depend on you being a leader with an all-encompassing vision (in a good way) and positive, life-changing solutions. A fabulous way to showcase your vision and your solutions is by becoming a brand publisher. Brand publishers share important information that connects them with their tribes in significant and meaningful ways, while inspiring and educating them at the same time, advancing the cause of both the publisher and the content consumer.

Content marketing and publishing involve many strategies, tactics, parts, and components, so I want to narrow in on a focus. I picked two areas of content marketing that I believe will make the greatest impact on your life and business. Before I go into any detail about those two areas, I'll share with you some common questions that are asked of me—in one form or another—in my work as a content marketing expert, along with my one sincere and heart-felt answer.

Q: *What activity could I do that will push me to the top quickly in my profession (or niche)?*

Q: *How can I be seen as an experienced or leading expert in circles where I may not be very well known?*

Q: *How can I more easily get in front of audiences of qualified potential clients?*

Q: *What will help me gain real influence with opinion leaders, decision makers, and my most desirable, potential clients?*

Q: *What will cause influential people to want to connect and even partner with me?*

My empathic answer: *publish a digital magazine and author a book!*

Publishing a digital magazine and writing and publishing a book offer you two big bangs for your influence-marketing buck. I am eager to give you great information to help you embrace these two types of content marketing, along with a few sure-fire tips so you can take action on them right away.

I submit them to you as viable suggestions that I hope you will seriously consider.

You're a Leader Who Publishes!

A leader leads. Others look to a leader for definitive direction and solid answers. True leaders are motivated by a clear vision. They push towards change, and they want to improve the condition or state of a specific group of people. Their vision moves them daily—they see "it" as if "it" already was. They also have a compelling mission and "story"—often based on their own personal experiences—that drives them to make that vision into a reality for themselves and those they lead. Today, *you* can be that leader who creates, publishes, and distributes relevant, quality content that stems from your story (brand), and that's designed to help a clearly defined target audience.

Being a leader means you know precisely who you are leading and why. You know their desires, their struggles, their hopes, their tastes, their compulsions, their temptations, their insecurities, their weaknesses, and their strengths. You also know how to speak to them in a way that catches their attention and jiggles their interest, so you can assist them in taking needed action for desirable change. **Your book** and ***your digital magazine*** are the big-bang vehicles for your unique branded voice to tell and re-tell your motivating, brand-story, to reach and inspire those you have a passion to help.

A Digital Magazine—What's *That*?

A digital magazine is similar to an ebook in that it is simply a PDF with text and images, but it becomes a "magazine" by the layout and style, which is usually bold and colorful, with short articles and clever titles. The skillful use of design elements such as bullets, white space, text wrap, eye-catching photos, and a myriad of font styles makes reading them seam like entertainment. People are easily drawn to them, and they have a very high perceived value. A digital magazine has tremendous marketing draw, and if it's geared directly to your target group, it is a force you can't deny! It gets the job done and gets attention without question.

Your Magazine's Written Mission

You are the publisher of your own magazine (play along with me), so what are you here to contribute, and to whom? Besides being a marketing tool to generate revenue, precisely why does your magazine exist and for what does it stand?

Who are your readers, and what compelling, irresistible idea do you want them to rally around? Perhaps it is high-fashion for young city-dwelling professionals who want to feel they are in control of their lives, or maybe the answer is healthy, happy, fun-filled lifestyle design for the new "kids" over fifty who are ready to experience a more awakened and purposeful journey! Answer in one statement the *who,* the *what,* and the *why*! Who are these readers, why will they read your publication, and what should they gain from your magazine? What do they want and how can you influence and improve their lives? Find the answers and create your *magazine's mission statement*. Then write it down (you may even use it as a tagline to your magazine's title). Memorize it. Hang it on your wall, poster-style! Then, be fully committed and faithfully dedicated to this purpose! From there, the planning and execution of each issue of your digital magazine is breezy: simply demonstrate, communicate, reiterate, substantiate, and authenticate this mission (an extension of your brand-story) in all the content you publish.

Two Big Bangs for Your Influence-Marketing Buck

Putting a Digital Magazine Issue Together

I want to mention that you can—if you felt like taking on the challenge—create your magazine pages in a program as basic as Microsoft Word, and convert the document to a PDF using Adobe or one of the many free PDF software downloads. This is as basic as it gets, but it will work. Or, if you have the budget and the resources, you can purchase professional software such as InDesign for your team members to use. Or, you can simply hire an outside professional (like my company) to do the magazine layout for you.

In order to communicate clearly to your reader and potential clients, and to strengthen your business brand, each issue of your magazine should have a theme that is decided upon by a well thought out set of business goals and objectives. Support the publication's theme throughout the entire issue.

Your digital magazine can be as simple or as elaborate as you are willing to make it, however, the more complex it is, the more time and money you will have to invest. I personally think simple is always best. There is something almost magical about an attractive publication with strong content and great visuals that's also clean and easy to read.

Don't complicate this production task by trying to create a *Super-Mag* your first time at bat. Keep pulling yourself back to simplicity whenever you're tempted to wander. Aim for a digital magazine of about twenty to thirty pages in length, plus the front and back covers. Your interior will have a table of contents, a "Letter from the Editor" (that's you), and eight to twelve strategic articles (about two pages each, or roughly 400-700 words each) that your list and subscribers would be excited to read, written by results-gaining influencers and experts who know their stuff. Leave room for a 50-75 word bio plus one URL for each of the writers at the end of their respective articles.

Your letter from the editor will stir up inspiration, and set the tone for the issue, sort of like a "keynote speech." Also include in the magazine a "featured" or "main" article (one of the eight to twelve) written by a strategic partner or team member, on a topic of very high interest to your readers.

Select one captivating image (your own high-quality shot or a licensed image, please) and an intriguing title for each article. Do the same for the front cover, where you will also add some tantalizing highlights—in various colored fonts—of what's inside. Reserve the back cover for a special sponsor or an advertiser, at top billing!

A Variety of Article Types

Add a dash of spice to your magazine by featuring a variety of article types. Here are just a few that could work for you:

- A new or clever way of doing a thing
- An article on "best-practices"
- An article on improving lifestyle
- A piece on "what leaders in the industry are saying"
- A "how-to" instruction
- An expert opinion on a current trend or issue

Two Big Bangs for Your Influence-Marketing Buck

- ◎ A tips list (8 tips for _____, 5 tips to_____)
- ◎ Information about upcoming events

Your Team

Fashion your team. You will need writers for the articles, a copywriter for your ads and announcements, a graphic designer and/or magazine layout expert to lay out the pages, and a proof reader to give it the once over after everything is put together. These helpers come at a price, of course. Perhaps you can wear a few of the necessary hats at first, until your budget opens up, but delegate the jobs as soon as possible. Your end product will be better when you delegate to the experts.

How Often to Publish

You may be wondering how often to publish your magazine. There is no ideal publishing frequency for every entrepreneur, but publish often enough to keep the momentum going, and spaced out enough so your reader is eagerly anticipating the next issue. Choose a frequency schedule and stick to it consistently.

At first you can publish it two to four times a year, and increase that if you feel the benefits and results you gain (in terms of new clients, increased sales, and new opportunities) are worth the effort and expense (of your time, your team, or your money).

Your Editorial Calendar Helps You Plan

Planning your magazine issues in advance will help you stay in control of your brand and your content, and allow you to carefully strategize the best way to serve your community while branding your content to your mission.

Through the use of an editorial calendar, planning becomes easy and organized, and each digital magazine issue forms into a cohesive whole. Your editorial calendar allows you a way to see the big picture and how each piece of content fits. It helps you synthesize and edit to produce a great product.

Lay out the editorial calendar of your magazine for an entire year in advance by selecting a theme for each issue, and deciding on your article topics as they relate to your business and revenue goals.

Decide on a main goal for each article: what do you want the reader to gain, know, or do after reading? Will you send them to a landing page for additional content related to the article? A clear call-to-action helps everyone.

Choose supportive materials for each theme, and decide who the writers will be to help you carry out your theme, plans, and goals. Then secure advertisers, and decide on which of your products, events, and services you will promote within the pages of each magazine, well before any issue is even in production.

Sign Me Up! A Free Gift on Your Site or Landing Page

Your *Valuable Free Gift* is quite often your first significant opportunity to begin a meaningful relationship with your prospect, and communicate your value through a clear message and purpose that is uniquely tied to your brand-story.

Your *Valuable Free Gift* will normally be some type of highly beneficial and useful content designed to help your visitor accomplish an important goal, solve an annoying problem, or gain a desired outcome. It is often something that's delivered digitally, like a report, checklist, or audio.

Certainly your digital magazine can be a stand-alone piece of valuable content you generously gift (or sell) to your community, but it can also make a splendid *Valuable Free Gift*, that few of your competitors can touch!

Social Media and Your Mag

Create dedicated social media pages for your magazine on at least two or three social sharing sites that are relevant to your readers. LinkedIn would be a great match for a business magazine. Posts from an interior design publication (which would be highly visual in nature), would be fitting on Pinterest. A brand or product page on Facebook is ideal for a magazine, as would be a group where people could converse and interact around each issue.

Keep your posts and tweets short and sweet, and pair them with a tip right out of your current issue. Invite people to sign up on the spot, particularly if the magazine is free of charge. Your posts can lead them directly to the sign-up page.

Every time a new issue comes out, let your Facebook friends and Twitter followers know it. Share the link on Google + too, since everyone enjoys a recreational and educational read. Tag the article writers and editors, so they can share the good news, too, Twitter is the perfect platform to tweet one-liners from each issue. Don't forget to @YourMagazine!

Magazines are blogalicious! If you produce four issues of your magazine each year, you would never be in need of blog content again! Blog about the various articles in each issue, or feature one of the writers. Just one magazine issue could give you enough blog content for a month or two, or even more.

Mag Tools

Let me conclude this section on digital magazines with a list of a few helpful tools and resources you can use to get going fast and with flair. Check them out to see if they are right for you.

Elance—Through Elance you can hire freelancers—including moderately-priced designers—to help with your magazine layout and images. You can also use Elance to find proofreaders and graphic artists. http://www.Elance.com

Cute PDF—This is a free program that's available online to quickly turn your Word document into a handy PDF. http://www.CutePDF.com

issuu—A free (and paid) online tool that will not only turn your Word document into a PDF, it will create a "flipbook" style of magazine with page-flip animation, and even host it as well! All you have to do is sign up, upload your document, convert it, and share the link with your community, and issuu also supports magazines with audio, video, social sharing, and responsive content. Go to issuu to also view other digital magazines for inspiration and style ideas. Make a note of which ones attract you and why. http://www.issuu.com

Flipb—Purchase and use this software to create flip-book publications. It will convert your PDF into a flipbook in minutes! The software is available for Windows and Mac. http://flipb.com

Adobe Creative Cloud—This a convenient, cloud-based subscription plan that gives you and your team members 24/7 access to the most popular Adobe programs, including Photoshop, Illustrator, InDesign, and more, so you can create a state-of-the-art publication. http://www.adobe.com

3D Issue—You can publish interactive digital magazines and a variety of branded Apps with this online software. http://www.3dissue.com

DreamsTime—Here you can purchase the license for images and footage you can use in your publication. Some are even free. http://www.Dreamstime.com

A Book of Your Own—Become a Published Author

The single most significant thing you can do to advance your business and career, and to stand out as a leader in your profession is to author a book. As an author, I write books.

When you become an author, you gain instant respect, and with it you often gain a clear, competitive advantage, especially if you have written about a key issue or concern surrounding the people in your niche, and offered great solutions that work.

As a book publisher and content marketing expert, I publish books for other professionals and business owners through my publishing house, *Splendor Publishing* (we are the publisher of the book you are reading right now)! If you want to become visible and influential, write and publish your book!

I find it extremely rewarding to help my clients create their books, because I see how quickly it increases their confidence levels, and takes them to the next level. If you need help with the book writing and publishing process, I am here to help. The point is . . . just write it!

Don't wait any longer to start writing your book. I give you some great tips below for creating an outline so you can get started soon. I bet you already have a concept or book title floating around in your head. I'll bet you even have content just "sitting" around on your computer— such as audios you can have transcribed, or speech notes you can expand upon—that could easily become a book with some TLC,.

If taking on an entire book right now seems like a stretch, consider co-authoring with another professional, preferable someone with influence in your field. Or, gather together a group of colleagues who desire more influence, and co-author an anthology similar to this one, where each person writes just one chapter. I help entrepreneurs do this all the time. It's the quickest way to author a book. Contact me and I'll show you how you can publish a group book at no cost to you, with your name on the front cover as the compiler or main author!

A Formula to Write Your Book in Twelve Weeks Flat!

Do you want to write a non-fiction book (self-help, business, personal development), but feel you need guidance to put together your manuscript? Well you don't have to envy other authors ever again. *You* can write your book quickly, and get *your* life-changing message to the world. Yes, you can get *your* book published! I want to help you become an author—maybe a best-selling author—with the very simple writing guide below!

I work with a lot of writers and best-selling authors, and most them felt stuck or overwhelmed at some point in the writing process, so you are not alone. These feelings are easily overcome with a simple writing plan.

Two Big Bangs for Your Influence-Marketing Buck

You can stay on track with your writing, and actually complete your manuscript in weeks or months, not years, with my easy book-writing formula and schedule. Here it is:

1. Create a "working title" for your book. Right now this may be as "raw" as a general topic of interest along with a short description of what you want to write about relative to that topic. That's OK. This is just your working title to help you focus on the rest of the formula. It's all good! Write it down.

2. Pick up your pen again, and brainstorm a list of your chapters. These are the main topic categories you want to cover in the book. Just use working titles for now and don't get stuck on figuring out your actual chapter titles. Aim for twelve chapters (of which one will be an introduction and one a conclusion).

3. For *each* of the twelve working chapters on your list, jot down three sub-headings that will support the main point of that chapter. As you did when brainstorming your list of chapters, use "working" heading names (placeholder headings). The actual heading names can be fine-tuned and finalized later, after you have done your writing.

4. Now write your book one heading at a time, using **Splendor Publishing**'s *12-Week Book-Writing Schedule* (what you are reading right now). Tackle one chapter at a time. Each week for twelve weeks, write three 1200-word "articles" (three articles for each chapter of your book).

In addition, each week for twelve weeks you will:

- Take a few minutes each Sunday to go over your writing plan for the coming week and to mentally prepare. Chose one of the twelve chapters to focus on, along with that chapter's three headings. Then write an introduction paragraph for that chapter (200-400 words or so).

- Next, you will write the content for one chapter heading on Monday, one heading on Wednesday, and one heading on Friday. These are the 1200-word "articles."

- Repeat this routine every week for twelve weeks. In just three months you will have completed the entire manuscript for your book!

Super Bonus Tip: You do not necessarily have to write your chapters in the order they will appear in your book. Go with your natural writing flow and tendency. Each Sunday, choose the chapter you feel most in the "mood" to tackle for the coming week.

Your Book . . . An Industry Classic?

Can your book become the to go-to-book for your profession? Why not? If you do the research, answer the most burning questions of the clients in your industry, and provide real and measurable solutions to bring about significant life or business improvements, you have the inputs for an industry classic. Write with a mission, a purpose, and a plan, and base the content on a well thought out outline. Then, get a talented

Two Big Bangs for Your Influence-Marketing Buck

cover designer, a skilled editor, and a meticulous proof reader, and your book will be rock solid and ready for Amazon and bookstore shelves.

30 Steps to Self Publish Your Paperback Book

Of course I would love to speak with you about **Splendor Publishing** producing and marketing your book. However, I know that some people want to attempt this for themselves, and that person may be you. If it is *not*, then certainly contact me at Margo@MargoDeGange.com so we can chat. If you are that person who is ready to do this alone, I have made a list for you of the major steps involved. Without going into detail for each one (that's an entire book in itself), here are the general steps to create and publish your printed paperback book for print-on-demand publishing (the steps are not necessarily in exact order. The order will be based on how you and your team function):

1. Decide when (month and year) you want to publish your book.

2. Create a basic outline for your book with a working title and working chapter topics (use the formula I shared in this chapter).

3. Write the manuscript from the outline.

4. Fine tune the book title, chapter titles, and headings.

5. Secure your ISBN.

6. Purchase your bar code (for distribution through retailers).

7. Create the front matter for your manuscript (and many of these pages are optional), including the half title page, title page, copyright page, dedication, table of contents, foreword, preface, acknowledgements, and introduction (sometimes the introduction is more like a chapter, and therefore not part of the front matter, but rather part of the book's body).

8. Create the back matter of your book, which may include an index, a glossary, and various other pieces that are not part of the main body of the book.

9. Edit your manuscript (may include style editing, copy editing, and general editing).

10. Proof read your manuscript.

11. Create your book's description to use for book listings, for marketing, for the cover of your endorsement request letters, and possibly, for placement on the back cover.

12. Send out a sample of the manuscript along with an endorsement request letter, to secure book testimonials and endorsements.

13. Complete the interior layout process of your book to prepare it for printing. This includes properly setting up page breaks and pagination.

14. Do a second proof of the final draft after the interior layout is complete.

15. Design the cover of your book (includes three stages: design, artwork, and layout).

16. Register with the Library of Congress for a pre-assigned control number (LCCN or Library of Congress Control Number).

17. Register your book with Books in Print and other book agencies, book websites, and book listings.

18. Prepare your book files in proper PDF form—both your book's cover file and interior file—according to your printer's requirements.

19. Submit all of the book's information to the printer, which involves filling out all of the necessary forms and fields.

20. Submit or upload your files to the printer.

21. Order a hard-copy, physical proof of your completed book.

22. Approve your files with the printer if you are happy with the physical, hard-copy proof.

23. If you plan to sell your paperback book on Amazon (who wouldn't?), create and complete an Author Central author page for yourself, and add your book to your Author Central page.

24. Create a sales page or information page for your book on your website.

25. Prepare the marketing plan for your book, and put together the marketing activities and materials, which may include a book launch party, a virtual book launch, press releases, endorsements, banners, 3D digital book images, pre-written social media posts, video, newsletter copy, a sales page, etc.

26. When the book goes "live," market the heck out of it (you can even start marketing before it is live), and share the Amazon link with everyone on your mailing list and on social media.

27. Order a couple of copies of your own book directly from Amazon. Send the books to special friends and supporters as thank-you gifts.

28. Place a wholesale order for books. These are the copies that you can bring with you to sell at your speaking events, or that you can give away to colleagues and clients.

29. Secure media appearances as the interesting and knowledgeable author who you are.

30. Get a cup of your favorite tea, and maybe a cookie, and leisurely read your own book. Better yet, have someone take a photo of you leisurely reading your one book and share it on social media!

Note: *This list will help you through the general steps to produce your print-on-demand paperback book. You will definitely also want to produce an ebook version of your book, which will include a Kindle version and perhaps some others. The process for creating an ebook or digital book is different from the steps listed above. In addition, the interior files are different too. You will also need an ISBN for each version of your book (hardcover, paperback, ebook, audio book, etc).*

If publishing a book seems like a time consuming process, with a long list of many steps, that's because it is! You don't create a book in a weekend—not a quality book you will be proud to bring into professional circles. Don't settle for a book that looks homemade and that is not created and structured for solid networking and marketing. Give yourself several months for the entire process (or more). If, after giving this list some consideration, you still feel the task of publishing your own book is too great, you may certainly give me a shout out. We can help you by taking your manuscript and getting it ready for print, and completing for you all of the behind-the-scenes work and tasks listed here. Or, you may want to do *a few* of the tasks yourself, *but not all*. Still, we are here to help with that.

Contact me for a chat. I'm friendly and fun to talk with, I must admit! So don't be shy. I want to hear all about your passion and your vision for your book. I look forward to hearing how your project or plan is coming along.

Margo DeGange, M.Ed., *Speaker, Author, Publisher*

INTENTIONAL CONTENT MARKETING FOR ENTREPRENEURS ON A MISSION

Gain Influence, Visibility & Credibility . . . Publish Your Book, Advance Your Calling!

Margo's Special Offer:

Want to **Self Publish** Your Book,
but with Margo at Your Side?
Get ONE-HALF OFF Margo's Next
Book Brilliance Virtual Intensive
Learn More at
SplendorPublishing.com/book-brilliance

About Margo DeGange, M.Ed.

Content Marketing Strategist and non-fiction Book Publisher, Margo DeGange, M.Ed., is an international best-selling author and speaker, and founder of ***Splendor Publishing***, the publishing house dedicated to helping entrepreneurs become published authors quickly and with ease—and ***Women of Splendor***, the exciting faith-based business mentoring and networking organization where spiritually-minded women with important life-work collaborate to become wildly successful. Quarterly, Margo hosts the life-transforming 4-Seasons of Success conferences.

Known for radically inspirational business and lifestyle re-design, Margo can help you discover your authentic "Gift of Brilliance," then shine full throttle through content marketing from the heart!

Margo has written over twenty books and has produced a plethora of robust content for entrepreneurs and managed businesses, converting this activity into big sales and far-reaching networks. Much of her work has been in the coaching, speaking, online marketing, and interior design fields.

Margo will help you lead with a content plan to build your community and gain expert status, while adding tremendous value to your brand. She holds a Masters Degree in Adult Education & Instructional Design, with a focus in content creation and delivery, as well as degrees in Leadership & Communication, and Speech Communication.

In addition to consulting entrepreneurs and businesses managers, Margo's almost 30-year career includes content marketing strategy, content creation, and content publishing of: *books, seminars, done-for-you products, ezines, digital magazines, ebooks, podcasts, radio shows, presentations, speeches, print magazines, training manuals, digital & print articles, reports, surveys, membership sites, landing pages, contests, train-the-trainer programs, community programs, infographics, multiple-module courses, licensing programs, certification courses, and more.* She's created and taught hundreds of events, classes, webinars, and teleseminars worldwide.

. . . need a content strategy to build a loyal tribe, or a powerful vehicle to deliver it (book publishing, blogging, article marketing, pre-made seminars, etc.)? Margo is your go-to girl!

Facebook: Facebook.com/Margo.DeGange

Twitter: Twitter.com/MargoDeGange

Pinterest: Pinterest.com/MargoDeGange

LinkedIn: Linkedin.com/in/MargoDeGange

Email: Margo@MargoDeGange.com

**To find out more about Margo visit:
http://www.MargoDeGange.com,
http://www.WomenOfSplendor.com, and
http://www.SplendorPublishing.com**

Is there a book in you waiting to spring forth?
We would love to help you become a published author!

Splendor Publishing helps entrepreneurs and individuals with important life-work become published authors. Our books encourage personal, professional, and spiritual growth. *Splendor* books are written by experts who want to share their message with the world in a big and brilliant way!

We publish soft cover, hard cover, and digital books for popular readers and devices, in black and white or full color, with professionally designed covers you will be thrilled to present to your peers, clients, friends, and colleagues.

Nothing "reads" credibility and expert status like being a published author. Get better speaking engagements and greater media exposure, too.

Perhaps you're just in the idea stage, or you've begun writing your content. Or, maybe you may have no idea where or how to begin. No worries! ***Splendor Publishing*** will guide you each and every step of the way, to complete your own book, or even a group book project with two or more coauthors.

Whether you want to compile an anthology of many writers, write your own book to promote your business or ministry, or collaborate on a project for your non-profit or community organization, we can help. Our anthology books are fabulous for marketing, training or fund-raising.

Let us help you make your dream of being a published author a reality. Contact ***Splendor Publishing*** today, at 979-777-2229 or visit **http://www.SplendorPublishing.com.**

A Final Note from Tracy Repchuk

Thank you for your investment in this book, and for the continuing relationship you will have with me and the co-authors.

We are dedicated to serving you and your needs and look forward to our journey together with you. Remember to **claim *your free gifts*** at **www.StartRightMarketing.com** where all the author's gifts can be found in one place.

Enjoy the journey and stay in touch.

To Your Ongoing Success,

Tracy Repchuk
5-Time International Bestselling Author and Speaker
Get a Fully Branded End-to-End Website Presence in Under 60 Days!